In His Words
Readings from the Life of Abraham Lincoln

Charles M. Hubbard
Michael Toomey

Kendall Hunt
publishing company

Cover images:
Portrait of Abraham Lincoln:
Library of Congress Prints and Photographs Division [LC-DIG-ppmsca-19208].

Gettysburg Address, draft copy of John Hay:
Abraham Lincoln. "Hay Draft" of the Gettysburg Address, 1863. Manuscript. John Hay Papers, Manuscript Division, Library of Congress Digital ID # cw0127p1.

Kendall Hunt
publishing company

www.kendallhunt.com
Send all inquiries to:
4050 Westmark Drive
Dubuque, IA 52004-1840

Copyright © 2014 by Kendall Hunt Publishing Company

ISBN 978-1-4652-4069-9

All rights reserved. No part of this publication may be reproduced, stored in a retrieval system, or transmitted, in any form or by any means, electronic, mechanical, photocopying, recording, or otherwise, without the prior written permission of the copyright owner.

Printed in the United States of America
10 9 8 7 6 5 4 3 2 1

Contents

Introduction vii

Selected Events in the Life of Abraham Lincoln xi

PART ONE – Growing and Learning 1

Politics 3
- To the People of Sangamo County, March 9, 1832 4
- "The Perpetuation of Our Political Institutions" – Address to the Young Men's Lyceum of Springfield, Illinois, January 27, 1838 7

Courtship 14
- To Mary S. Owens, December 13, 1836 15
- To Mary Owens, May 7, 1837 16
- To Mary Owens, August 16, 1837 17
- Letter to Mrs. Orville Browning, April 1, 1838 18

Melancholy 21
- To John T. Stuart, January 20, 1841 22
- To John T. Stuart, January 23, 1841 23
- To Joshua F. Speed, January 3 [?], 1842 24
- To Joshua F. Speed, February 3, 1842 26

- To Joshua F. Speed [private], February 25, 1842 27
- To Joshua F. Speed, February 25, 1842 28
- To Joshua F. Speed, March 27, 1842 29

Accountability 31
- Letter from the Lost Townships [the "Rebecca Letter"], August 27, 1842 31
- To James Shields, September 17, 1842 37
- Memorandum of Duel Instructions to Elias H. Merryman, September 19, 1842 37
- To Joshua F. Speed, October 5, 1842 39

Principles 40
- To Martin S. Morris, March 26, 1843 40
- Handbill Replying to Charges of Infidelity, July 31, 1846 42
- Fragment: Notes for a Law Lecture, July 1, 1850 [?] 43
- To Joshua F. Speed, August 24, 1855 44
- To Isham Reavis, November 5, 1855 48

PART TWO – Lincoln and Slavery 49

Early Views 52
- Protest in the Illinois Legislature on Slavery, March 3, 1837 53
- To Mary Speed, September 27, 1841 54
- Remarks and Resolution Introduced in United States House of Representatives Concerning Abolition of Slavery in the District of Columbia 56
- Fragments on Slavery, April 1[?], 1854 58

Attacking Slavery 59
- Speech at Peoria, Illinois (excerpts), October 16, 1854 59
- To George Robertson, August 15, 1855 68
- "A House Divided": Speech at Springfield, Illinois, June 16, 1858 69
- Fourth Debate with Stephen A. Douglas at Charleston, Illinois, September 18, 1858 78
- Address at Cooper Institute, New York City, February 27, 1860 82

The End of Slavery 92
- Message to Congress, March 6, 1862 93
- Emancipation Proclamation, January 1, 1863 95
- Reply to New York Workingmen's Democratic Republican Association, March 21, 1864 97
- To Charles D. Robinson, August 17, 1864 99

PART THREE – Lincoln and the Presidency 103

Taking Charge 105
- Speech in Independence Hall, Philadelphia, Pennsylvania, February 22, 1861 106
- First Inaugural Address, March 4, 1861 107
- To William H. Seward, April 1, 1861 115
- Proclamation Suspending the Writ of *Habeas Corpus*, September 24 1862 116
- To the Workingmen of Manchester, England, January 19, 1863 117

Commander-in-Chief 119
- To John A. McClernand, November 10, 1861 120
- To George B. McClellan, June 28, 1862 121
- To William H. Seward, June 28, 1862 122
- To George B. McClellan, July 1, 1862 123
- To Joseph Hooker, January 26, 1863 123
- Letters to Joseph Hooker, June 10-16, 1863 124-128
- To Ulysses S. Grant, April 30, 1864 129

Explaining the Cost 129
- Meditation on the Divine Will, September 2, 1862 [?] 130
- To Fanny McCullough, December 23, 1862 131
- To Erastus Corning and Others, June 12, 1863 132
- Address Delivered at the Dedication of the Cemetery at Gettysburg, November 19, 1863 ... 140
- To Mrs. Lydia Bixby, November 21, 1864 141

Reunion and Reconciliation 142
- To Andrew Johnson, September 11, 1863 143
- Proclamation of Amnesty and Reconstruction, December 8, 1863 144
- To Michael Hahn, March 13. 1864 147
- Memorandum Concerning His Probable Failure of Re-election, August 23, 1864 147
- Second Inaugural Address, March 4, 1865 148
- Last Public Address, April 11, 1865 150

Acknowledgments

We would like to express our appreciation to our colleagues professors Rebecca Brackman and Debra Salata for proofreading the manuscript and offering suggestions to improve the organization and clarity. We are particularly indebted to our students at Lincoln Memorial University whose continuing interest in everything Lincoln enriches our teaching and research experience. We would also like to thank Taylor Hunsberger, Michelle Bahr, and the editorial staff at Kendall/Hunt for shepherding the manuscript through the production process.

Introduction

Gore Vidal, the well-known American novelist and playwright, described Abraham Lincoln as "a literary genius who was called upon to live, rather than merely to write, a high tragedy. I can think of no one in literary or political history quite like this essential American writer."[1] It is those essential qualities of Lincoln's writings—no less than the times in which he lived—that are reflected in the selections included in this book. Many of the selections are familiar while others are not, but taken together they illustrate Lincoln's growth from a youthful frontiersman into an accomplished attorney, political orator and, finally, president and commander-in-chief during the greatest constitutional and military crisis in American history. Lincoln's growth and transformation into one of America's most iconic historical figures is due in large part to his remarkable ability to communicate through the written and spoken word. The following documents represent only a small fraction of Lincoln's known works—there are more than 100,000 documents in the 10 volumes of Roy Basler's *Collected Works of Abraham Lincoln* and thousands of additional legal documents edited by Daniel Stowell in 2008.[2] But it is hoped that these documents provide some insight into the cultural and political life of the central figure in nineteenth century America.

Abraham Lincoln's election to the presidency of the United States in 1860 resulted largely from his remarkable talent and ability as a politician. These were skills he had developed through practical experience as a regional leader of the Whig Party and, later, as

---

1 Abraham Lincoln (Don E. Fehrenbacher, ed.), *Abraham Lincoln: Selected Speeches and Writings* (New York: Library of America, 2009 [1992]), xxvi – xxvii.
2 Roy Basler, ed., *The Collected Works of Abraham Lincoln*, 10 vols. (New Brunswick, NJ: Rutgers University Press, 1953); Daniel W. Stowell, ed., *The Papers of Abraham Lincoln: Legal Documents and Cases*, 4 vols. (Charlottesville: University of Virginia Press, 2008).

a member of the new Republican Party. The strength of the Republicans was in the free states of the North and their appearance came at a time when the country was deeply divided and fractured along regional, cultural, and certainly political lines. Lincoln's election exacerbated the difficulties already prevailing in the political landscape and resulted in the rapid secession of the cotton states of the lower South. During the winter of 1860-61, the secession crisis worsened and by the time of his inauguration Lincoln was confronted with open rebellion. Seven states had already severed their ties to the Union, and it appeared that the country had literally come apart.

Lincoln believed that secession was unconstitutional and that his first task was to defend the integrity of the Constitution. If necessary he was prepared to use force to maintain national authority, just as the seceded states were willing to fight to gain their independence. And so, in Lincoln's words, "the war came." Lincoln is the only president in American history whose entire presidency from beginning to end was engaged in war. Ultimately, war defined his presidency and, it is often said, made it possible for Lincoln to reunite the country and restore the union. There is some truth in that statement, but for Lincoln, the war was not about restoring the Union; in his view the Union was never destroyed. He refused to recognize the legitimacy of the rebels or their right to secede. From the outbreak of hostilities Lincoln's military objective was to destroy the rebel army and restore the authority of the central government. But Lincoln also hated slavery and ultimately the military necessities of war enabled him to bring about the end of that institution in the United States. Despite early military setbacks, Lincoln remained resolute and determined to prosecute the war until victory was achieved. Lincoln understood and accepted his responsibilities as president and commander-in-chief and his words clearly demonstrate his involvement in military strategy and tactics. Moreover, the power of Lincoln's spoken and written words enabled him to rally public opinion to believe in the cause and ultimately mobilize the nation's resources to support the Army.

The following collection of documents is drawn from letters, speeches, and transcripts, all of which can be directly and accurately ascribed to Lincoln. Lincoln's written words survive, for the most part, in original documents, either written in his own hand or verified as accurate copies by Lincoln's signature and, sometimes, with his marginal notes. Public speeches are also considered original because they were transcribed and reproduced in newspapers or pamphlets soon after they were spoken. A number of original Lincoln documents, particularly during his presidency, were copied by his secretary, John Hay, and are therefore considered Lincoln's words.[3] These documents provide unparalleled insight into Lincoln's growth as a lawyer and politician, and especially about his four years as president.

Regrettably, however, they give less information about his childhood or personal life. Lincoln wrote very little about his early years. Indeed, much of what we know about his childhood and early life is based on the recollections and memories of people who knew him, either personally or by reputation. Lincoln also rarely referenced his emotional state in writings as a young adult. There is, for example, overwhelming evidence that Lincoln struggled with moods of depression or melancholy, but his written words contain only a few references to this complex emotional condition. Lincoln comes closest to revealing his profound depression in a series of letters to Joshua Speed. These letters were written in the aftermath of Lincoln's traumatic breakup with Mary Todd in January 1841 and they offer a rare glimpse into Lincoln's personal feelings. But it is nothing more than a glimpse. This and other seemingly well-

---

3 Don E. Fehrenbacher, *Recollected Words of Abraham Lincoln* (Redwood City, CA: Stanford University Press, 1996), xliii – liv; see especially p. l-li.

known facets of Lincoln's early years can never be verified through the acid test of Lincoln's own words, because Lincoln was reluctant in his youth, and throughout his life, to reveal his innermost thoughts and fears. He was outgoing and anxious to interact with people, but Lincoln remained an extraordinarily private person throughout his life.[4]

Because Lincoln was reluctant to share his feelings, we have very few words to help us understand Lincoln's views on religion. Those writings that we do have are often ambiguous and at times almost cynical. Lincoln undoubtedly rejected the emotionalism associated with the Baptist Church that his father, Thomas, attended with the family in Indiana. However the evidence suggests that Lincoln did embrace a certain Calvinistic version of predestination that translated into a sense of fatalism. Mary Todd Lincoln said of her husband, "Mr. Lincoln's maxim and philosophy was—'what is to be, will be, and no prayers of ours can arrest the decree.'"[5] Lincoln believed that God was active in human affairs and ultimately controlled the fate of humanity. Lincoln's words in his second inaugural address express his spiritual feelings. Indeed, it was his acceptance of a naturalistic approach to predestination and determinism that allowed him to shoulder the responsibilities of the horrific casualties and destruction of the Civil War.

That Lincoln chose not to share his personal feelings with others does not negate the fact that he was a brilliant and effective communicator of complex ideas. Over the years, he attributed his clarity of thinking and his remarkable memory to the practice of recording things he read and thought about. Lincoln cultivated a lifelong habit of writing his thoughts down on paper. He frequently wrote out exact passages or paraphrases of his reading. He once told a friend in New Salem that "the way he learned to write so well and so distinctly and precisely was by writing friendly confidential letters."[6] Unfortunately, many of these early letters have not survived because they were written, for the most part, as favors for illiterate neighbors who wanted to correspond with their family and friends. But Lincoln continued this practice during his presidency to clarify his thinking, and many of the notes he used for this purpose were incorporated into his major speeches and documents.

Such a disciplined effort resulted in a unique and effective writing style that came to maturity under the most trying of circumstances. It was a style that often relied on familiar literature, as, for example, when Lincoln paraphrased from the book of Matthew in the King James Version of the Bible for his famous "House Divided" speech. He read and memorized Shakespeare's classics and the passion so often contained in Lincoln's words reflect his familiarity with the famous English playwright. Moreover, Lincoln's literary versatility can be observed in technical and well-organized legal and political arguments that he used frequently in court and in political debates. Lincoln's words are powerful, logical, and passionate and above all, well chosen. By the time his writing style was fully developed, he had become one of America's greatest wordsmiths.

This collection is not designed as a documentary biography, but every effort is made to provide documentary evidence highlighting fascinating and historically-relevant features of Lincoln's experience as a young man on the frontier, as a husband and father, as a successful Illinois lawyer, and

---

[4] Joshua Shenk, *Lincoln's Melancholy: How Depression Challenged a President and Fueled His Greatness* (New York: Houghton Mifflin Co., 2005), 3.
[5] William H. Herndon, "Lincoln's Religion," *Illinois State Register* (December 1873), cited in Douglas L. Wilson, "William H. Herndon and Mary Todd Lincoln," *Journal of the Abraham Lincoln Association* 22:2 (Summer 2001), accessed at http://quod.lib.umich.edu/j/jala
[6] Edward Dicey, "Washington During the War," *Macmillan's Magazine* (May 1862), 24.

ultimately as the political leader who guided the nation through the crucible of the Civil War. His words and actions convinced the American people not only to persevere and save the Union, but to create at the same time a more perfect union that granted freedom and liberty for all its citizens. His vision and conviction that the cause was worth fighting and dying for was powerfully communicated, not only to Americans, but to all humanity. Through a careful reading of his words, one can feel the passion and energy of what Lincoln called his "honest calling." From his earliest musings, writings, and public statements we can observe the development of his character and the essence of the very real and complex Abraham Lincoln.

The following pages contain letters, speeches, fragmentary notes, and other writings that portray the wide range and depth of Lincoln's thoughts and positions on a variety of personal and public issues. The documents are arranged in three sections that focus on important aspects of Lincoln's life, then further divided into thematic groupings. The entire collection is more or less chronological, although necessarily there is some overlap. We have included introductions to each section and to each grouping in order to provide context for the documents, but we have not included headers for the documents themselves. As much as possible, Lincoln's words can, and should, stand alone. Although some of the more recognizable speeches and documents are abridged for sake of brevity and emphasis, most of the documents are complete. In a few instances, we include notes and fragments of Lincoln's writings that were written in preparation for speeches or further correspondence. Where possible, we have remained faithful to Lincoln's words by retaining his punctuation and capitalization because these were devices used by Lincoln himself; modified punctuation, underlining, and other techniques were placed in the text by Lincoln to make his oral presentation more effective. Thus, we try to provide a sense of the passion and emotion Lincoln conveyed in his words.[7]

There is no way to convey the tangible connection to the author himself that comes from the thrill and excitement of holding and reading an original Lincoln document. That is an experience that only a select group of archivists and historians will ever know. Fortunately, the Library of Congress has made available digital copies of many of Lincoln's letters, speeches, and other documents, written in his own hand and often including his corrections, personalized punctuation, and notes.[8] Looking through this immense collection, it is readily apparent that Lincoln was a consummate writer who understood the importance of a well-chosen word. Ultimately, we hope that the limited collection offered here will accomplish a similar purpose and illustrate, through Lincoln's words, the complex and fascinating character of America's most essential leader.

---

[7] Douglas L. Wilson, *Lincoln's Sword: The Presidency and the Power of Words* (New York: Alfred A. Knopf, 2006); see especially 3-9.

[8] http://memory.loc.gov/ammem/alhtml/malhome.html. In addition to the digitized copies of Lincoln documents at the Library of Congress, extensive collections of transcribed and annotated documents are contained in the Basler collection referenced earlier, and in Don E. Fehrenbacher, ed., *Abraham Lincoln: Speeches and Writings, 1832-1865*, 2 vols (New York: The Library of America, 2013).

SELECTED EVENTS IN THE LIFE OF ABRAHAM LINCOLN

1809 February
- Abraham Lincoln is born in Hardin County, Kentucky.

1816 December
- The Lincoln family moves to Indiana, settling on Little Pigeon Creek in what is now Spencer County.

1818 October
- Nancy Hanks Lincoln, Abraham Lincoln's mother, dies of "milk-sickness."

1819 December
- Thomas Lincoln, Abraham Lincoln's father, marries Sarah Bush Johnston.

1830 Spring
- Thomas Lincoln moves to Macon County, Illinois, and shortly afterward to Coles County.

1831 July
- Lincoln leaves his father's farm, moves to New Salem on the Sangamon River.

1832 March
- Lincoln launches his first political campaign, a run for a seat in the Illinois state legislature.

April
- Lincoln enlists in the state militia as a volunteer in the Black Hawk War.

August
- Lincoln is defeated in his race for the legislature.

1833 Autumn
- Lincoln is briefly introduced to Mary Owens.

1834 August
- Lincoln is elected to the Illinois state legislature and begins to study law after encouragement from John Todd Stuart, an attorney and fellow legislator.

1835 August
- Ann Rutledge, with whom Lincoln may have had a romantic relationship, dies from what was probably typhoid fever.

1836 August
- Lincoln is re-elected to the legislature.

September

- Lincoln is certified to practice law.

Autumn

- Mary Owens returns to New Salem and Lincoln begins an awkward courtship that lasts for about a year.

1837 March

- Lincoln introduces his first known formal opposition to the institution of slavery in a resolution in the Illinois legislature.

April

- Lincoln moves to Springfield; begins partnership with John Todd Stuart, meets and becomes friends with Joshua Speed.

August

- Lincoln writes his last letter to Mary Owens and it is apparently never answered.
- Mary Todd, on a brief visit to Springfield, is introduced to Lincoln.

1838 January

- In one of his earliest extensive public speeches, Lincoln addresses the Young Men's Lyceum of Springfield and outlines his belief that slavery is a threat to the federal government.

April

- Lincoln writes to Mrs. Orville Browning and recounts his failed relationship with Mary Owens.

August

- Lincoln is re-elected to a third term in the state legislature.

1839 October

- Mary Todd returns to Springfield to live with her sister.

1840 August

- Lincoln is elected to his fourth and last term in the Illinois legislature.

December

- Lincoln and Mary Todd are engaged.

1841 January

- Lincoln abruptly breaks off his engagement to Mary Todd and falls into a serious depression. Lincoln describes his condition in a letter to John Todd Stuart.

September

- Lincoln writes to Joshua Speed's sister in which he describes seeing several slaves shackled together on a steamboat and headed to the Deep South.

1842 January

- Lincoln writes the first in a series of personal letters to Joshua Speed, in which the two exchange ideas and concerns about marriage and other personal issues.

August

- Lincoln's "Rebecca Letter" is published in the local paper and causes James Shields, a political opponent, to challenge him to a duel.

September

- Lincoln and Shields meet but agree at the last minute to forego their duel.
- Lincoln and Mary Todd renew their courtship.

November

- Lincoln and Mary Todd are married.

1846 May

- Lincoln is nominated to run for a seat in the United States House of Representatives.

July

- Lincoln responds to charges of infidelity during his campaign.

August

- Lincoln is elected to Congress.

1847 December

- Lincoln introduces the "Spot Resolutions" in Congress but receives little support.

1849 January

- Lincoln introduces a resolution to abolish slavery in the District of Columbia but again receives very little support.

March

- Lincoln's term in Congress comes to an end.

April

- Lincoln returns to Springfield and lobbies unsuccessfully for a federal appointment from the Taylor administration.
- Uncertain of his political future, Lincoln effectively retires from politics and focuses instead on his legal career.

1850   February

- Lincoln's second-born son, Edward Baker, dies.

1851   January

- Thomas Lincoln, Abraham Lincoln's father, dies.

1854   April

- As the national debate over slavery intensifies, Lincoln resumes political activity and begins to refine his opposition to slavery.

May

- The Kansas-Nebraska Act is signed into law; Lincoln determines to seek political office in order to oppose the act.

October

- In Peoria, Lincoln delivers his most extensive speech yet in opposition to the Kansas-Nebraska Act.

1855   August

- In a letter to George Robertson, Lincoln displays an early version of his argument that the nation cannot survive if it remains divided on the issue of slavery.
- In a letter to Joshua Speed, Lincoln expresses uncertainty about his own political affiliation.

1856   May

- Lincoln becomes active in the Republican Party.

1858   May

- Lincoln is nominated to run against Stephen Douglas, sponsor of the Kansas-Nebraska Act, for a seat in the United States Senate. In accepting the nomination he delivers the "House Divided" speech in the Illinois statehouse.

August

- Lincoln and Douglas meet for the first two debates in a series they have agreed will include a total of seven debates.

September

- Two more debates are held; during the fourth debate in Charleston, Lincoln responds to charges that he favors Black equality.

October

- The final three debates are held.

November

- The legislature returns a narrow majority of Democrats, thus ensuring that Douglas will be re-elected to his Senate seat.

1860 February

- Lincoln delivers a speech at Cooper Union Hall in New York City in which he reinforces his opposition to the spread of slavery and presents himself as a moderate alternative to the more radical Republican candidates.

May

- Lincoln is nominated by the Illinois legislature as a candidate for president, and is subsequently nominated by the Republican Party as its presidential candidate.

November

- Lincoln is elected president.

December

- South Carolina becomes the first Southern state to secede from the Union.

1861 January

- Mississippi, Florida, Alabama and Georgia secede.

February

- Lincoln departs Springfield for Washington, taking a circuitous route that includes speeches and presentations at several cities along the way.
- Louisiana and Texas secede.

March

- Lincoln is inaugurated, and delivers his first inaugural address.

April

- In a letter to Secretary of State William Seward, Lincoln asserts his intention as commander-in-chief to set policy.
- Fort Sumter in Charleston harbor, the last significant federal installation in the South, is attacked by the Confederate military and forced to surrender.
- Lincoln responds with a call for 75,000 volunteers to put down the rebellion, places a naval blockade of the South, and issues a limited suspension of *Habeas corpus*.

May

- Virginia, Arkansas, and North Carolina, secede.

June

- Tennessee secedes.

July

- The first major battle of the war takes place at Manassas Junction in Virginia and is a defeat for the Federal forces.

November

- Lincoln becomes aware that his responsibilities as commander-in-chief will require him to respond to a wide range of complaints and demands from his commanding generals.

1862 February

- William Wallace Lincoln ("Willie"), the third child of Abraham and Mary Lincoln, dies in the White House.

March

- In his message to Congress, Lincoln recommends compensated emancipation as a way to encourage southern states back into the Union.

April

- In Virginia, General George B. McClellan, in command of the Union Army of the Potomac, begins his Peninsula Campaign after much delay.

June

- McClellan is attacked in front of Richmond and begins to retreat.

September

- In the aftermath of continued military setbacks, Lincoln expresses confusion as to why the "divine will" permits such a costly war to continue.
- The Battle of Antietam forces an invading Confederate army to retreat and gives Lincoln the opportunity to issue a preliminary Emancipation Proclamation.
- Lincoln expands the suspension of *Habeas corpus* to the entire nation.

December

- Major General Ambrose E. Burnside, now in command of the Army of the Potomac, attacks Fredericksburg and is repulsed with heavy losses.
- In his message to Congress, Lincoln shows that he is still unclear as to how best to end slavery and discusses such ideas as compensated emancipation and colonization.
- Congress passes a bill in support of Lincoln's nationwide suspension of *Habeas corpus*.
- In a letter to a young girl mourning the loss of her father in battle, Lincoln shows that he too has suffered loss and depression.

1863 January

- Lincoln signs the Emancipation Proclamation.
- Major General Joseph Hooker is appointed to command the Union Army of the Potomac.

May

- Hooker is defeated at Chancellorsville.

June

- Confederate commander Robert E. Lee begins a second invasion of the North.
- In a series of letters to Joseph Hooker, Lincoln shows that he has learned a great deal about military strategy.
- In a letter clearly intended for publication, Lincoln responds to accusations that he is exercising his executive powers too broadly.

July

- Lee's invading Confederate army attacks Union forces, now commanded by Major General George G. Meade, and is defeated after three days of fighting at Gettysburg.
- Vicksburg, Mississippi surrenders to Union general Ulysses S. Grant.

September

- In a letter to Andrew Johnson, military governor of Tennessee, Lincoln demonstrates his urgency in reestablishing loyal state governments as quickly as possible.

November

- Lincoln delivers the Gettysburg Address.
- A series of battle around Chattanooga results in another victory for Grant, and Lincoln brings him to Washington to assume command of all Union armies.

December

- Lincoln's Proclamation of Amnesty and Reconstruction reveals his intentions for lenient treatment of former Confederates.

1864   March

- In a letter to Michael Hahn, recently elected governor of Louisiana, Lincoln urges him to implement some form of limited suffrage for Free Blacks.

June

- Lincoln is nominated to run for a second term as president but becomes increasingly pessimistic about his chances of success.

August

- In a letter to Charles Robinson, Lincoln explains his position on slavery, emancipation, and ending the war.
- Mobile is captured, the first in a string of military victories that will have a positive impact on Lincoln's re-election.

September

- Atlanta is captured.

October

- Sheridan gains control of the Shenandoah Valley.

November

- Lincoln is re-elected.
- In a letter to a grieving mother who has reportedly lost five sons in military service, Lincoln once again demonstrates that he understands the nature of loss and grief.

1865 February

- The Thirteenth Amendment is passed in the House of Representatives and sent to the states for ratification.

March

- Lincoln's second Inaugural Address urges a speedy end to the war and a lenient approach to reconstruction.

April

- Richmond is captured and Lee's army surrenders a few days later.
- Lincoln delivers his last public speech, in which he reminds the nation that it is time to begin the crucial task of Reconstruction and suggests the Louisiana government as a model. Three days later, Lincoln is shot and killed by an assassin.

Part One

Growing and Learning

In the early spring days of 1861, the nation was already divided and on the brink of civil war. As president, it fell to Abraham Lincoln to confront this crisis, yet it is safe to say that very few people on either side of the conflict saw in him the qualities of an effective leader. Lincoln had appeared on the national stage only a few years earlier and was seemingly unprepared to confront the challenges that lay ahead. His experience in federal government was limited to a single term in the House of Representatives and his military knowledge was so brief and insignificant that he himself had once joked about it. There was little indication of the man that we now know as Abraham Lincoln.

In fact, Lincoln was not entirely unprepared to lead the nation through the Civil War. It is true that he was going to learn much as he moved through the next four years, but it is also true that he had already learned a great deal about leadership and responsibility by that time. The process could be said to have started in earnest when he arrived in the rough little river town of New Salem, Illinois, in 1831. It was here that Lincoln definitively separated himself from the physically-demanding farm life on the frontiers of Indiana and Illinois, and began to craft a future in which he lived by his intellect rather than his brawn. The transformation was not easy and Lincoln himself had no real idea at first of what the finished product might look like. Gradually, however, the picture took shape as Lincoln progressed through a variety of roles and professions, first in New Salem where he was a handyman, store clerk, surveyor, postmaster, and politician; and then as a lawyer in the new state capital of Springfield, where he married and started a family. Lincoln's growth during these three decades, both professionally and emotionally, was remarkable. By the time he left Springfield in 1861 to assume the duties of President of the United States, Lincoln was hardly the same man.

The challenges that Lincoln overcame as a youth are well-known—the deaths of close family members, most notably his mother, a difficult and strained relationship with his father that neither of the two men ever tried to repair, and a rising ambition that was neither understood nor appreciated in the farming communities of Indiana and Illinois. While these were indeed significant obstacles for the young man to overcome, perhaps the greatest challenges were those that he faced after he made the decision to leave his father's farm and seek his own life in New Salem with no money and nothing more than a promise of employment. Lincoln quickly gained the trust of his neighbors and after he had been in town for less than a year was encouraged to run for a seat in the Illinois state legislature. At about the same time, Lincoln joined the state militia to fight in the Black Hawk War, and while he saw no combat, he was elected captain of his company, an unexpected honor that he later claimed was the most satisfying success of his life. Lincoln's decision to run for political office and his brief service in the state militia provided early indicators of the new direction that Lincoln saw for himself. Neither venture led to immediate success—he lost the election for the legislature and his military career came to a quiet end after three months—but Lincoln had identified himself as a rising leader of his small community. His next decision, however, was less impressive: he returned from his militia service and agreed to become co-owner of a small general store, despite the fact that it required him to accept a considerable amount of debt. When that venture failed, he found himself unemployed and at the mercy of his creditors.

Through the intervention of his neighbors, Lincoln was appointed postmaster of New Salem and deputy surveyor for Sangamon County, and in 1834 he ran once again for the state legislature. This time he won, and on the heels of that success made the surprising decision to study law. There was no guarantee of success either as a lawyer or as a politician, and his problems with debt were still unresolved. But Lincoln was at last able to see a life ahead of him that matched the life he had imagined for himself years before as an unhappy farm hand, daydreaming of a future that no one else seemed to understand.

When Lincoln eventually qualified to practice law in 1837, he left the dying town of New Salem and moved to the new state capital of Springfield. There he joined a law firm of John Todd Stuart and, as a politician of increasing prominence, he formulated and refined his views on law and politics. While Lincoln's professional career was thus taking shape, he continued to face challenges of a deeper, emotional nature. As he moved into the social circles frequented by politicians and lawyers, it was painfully obvious that Lincoln was a child of the frontier. He knew little of proper manners and any clothes that he wore seemed ill-fitted to his tall, gawky frame. Lincoln's resulting insecurities became especially noticeable in Springfield, where he confronted the possibility that his "experiment" as a lawyer might not be successful. He confided his fears to Joshua Speed, whose close friendship was a marked exception in Lincoln's life. Their relationship was all the more remarkable when their divergent backgrounds are considered; Speed had been raised on a Kentucky plantation where slavery was accepted; he was educated, financially secure, and socially active. None of these characteristics could be applied to Lincoln, yet they shared a sense of intellectual curiosity rare for that time and place. As young men, they came of age when the nation itself was seeking to redefine itself; fads and fashions from temperance to phrenology were topics of discussion, and Lincoln and Speed must have been aware of, and fascinated by, these national trends. But more important, Lincoln was able to share his feelings, failings, and fears with Speed; no one else in his life claimed that distinction.

Among the topics the two men discussed was marriage, and it is apparent that neither of them was comfortable with the prospect. Indeed, by that point Lincoln had already shown that his uncertainties were most pronounced when he attempted courtship. But attempt it he did, and ultimately his efforts resulted in marriage to Mary Todd, a young and outgoing daughter of a successful Lexington banker. The influence of Mary Todd on the life and career of Lincoln cannot be overstated. It was she who reminded him of the importance of proper etiquette and professional appearance. With her guidance, Lincoln's own innate abilities, and their mutual ambition, the couple gained prominence in Illinois society. Although a single term in the United States Congress failed to garner the accolades he had hoped for, Lincoln returned to Springfield in 1848 as an unequivocal success story. As a former Congressman who had also served four terms in the state legislature, Lincoln's place among the leaders of his political party was assured. His legal practice was likewise successful as he was well on his way to becoming the most highly paid corporate lawyer in the state.

Had he chosen to do so, Lincoln might have allowed himself to sink into the comfortable role of a respected local politician and prosperous attorney. It would not have been surprising if he had made such a choice, particularly given the humble origins of his youth that he had overcome to achieve success, and there are some indications that he was prepared to accept that course. But Lincoln's ambition still simmered, and national events were quickly moving toward a crisis that would once again drive him into the political arena.

POLITICS

Almost every decision that Lincoln made during the first momentous year on his own was bound to have a profound influence on his future. None was more momentous than his decision in the early months of 1832 to seek political office. Lincoln lost that election—in fact, he had lost badly—but the process awakened a latent talent for politics that ultimately carried him to the White House. He soon became a leader of his political party and a master of the political process. During his first few years in politics, however, Lincoln developed and defined his ideas and his values, as seen in the following two documents. In "To the People of Sangamo County"—his first political statement—Lincoln introduces himself to the voters and at the same time, reveals his own motivations for entering politics. Six years later, in his "Address to the Young Men's Lyceum of Springfield," Lincoln refers to a recent mob attack in St. Louis to discuss the importance of respect for the law and to speculate on the consequences when that respect has eroded. All the fundamental components of Lincoln's worldview are presented here. The clean, precise style and lofty ideas that eventually came to characterize his writing were still in the future, but even so Lincoln clearly demonstrates that he has already progressed well beyond the level of local politics.

To the People of Sangamo County, March 9, 1832

Fellow Citizens: Having become a candidate for the honorable office of one of your representatives in the next General Assembly of this state, in accordance with an established custom, and the principles of true republicanism, it becomes my duty to make known to you - the people whom I propose to represent - my sentiments with regard to local affairs.

Time and experience have verified to a demonstration, the public utility of internal improvements. That the poorest and most thinly populated countries would be greatly benefitted by the opening of good roads, and in the clearing of navigable streams within their limits, is what no person will deny. But yet it is folly to undertake works of this or any other kind, without first knowing that we are able to finish them - as half-finished work generally proves to be labor lost. There cannot justly be any objection to having railroads and canals, any more than to other good things, provided they cost nothing. The only objection is to paying for them; and the objection to paying arises from the want of ability to pay.

With respect to the county of Sangamo, some more easy means of communication than we now possess, for the purpose of facilitating the task of exporting the surplus products of its fertile soil, and importing necessary articles from abroad, are indispensably necessary. A meeting has been held of the citizens of Jacksonville, and the adjacent country, for the purpose of deliberating and enquiring into the expediency of constructing a railroad from some eligible point on the Illinois River, through the town of Jacksonville, in Morgan County, to the town of Springfield, in Sangamo County. This is, indeed, a very desirable object. No other improvement that reason will justify us in hoping for, can equal in utility the railroad. It is a never-failing source of communication, between places of business remotely situated from each other. Upon the railroad the regular progress of commercial intercourse is not interrupted by either high or low water, or freezing weather, which are the principal difficulties that render our future hopes of water communication precarious and uncertain. Yet, however desirable an object the construction of a railroad through our country may be; however high our imaginations may be heated at the thought of it - there is always a heart-appalling shock accompanying the account of its cost, which forces us to shrink from our pleasant anticipations. The probable cost of this contemplated railroad is estimated at $290,000; the bare statement of which, in my opinion, is sufficient to justify the belief, that the improvement of Sangamo River is an object much better suited to our infant resources.

Respecting this view, I think I may say, without fear of being contradicted, that its navigation may be rendered completely practicable, as high as the mouth of the South Fork, or probably higher, to vessels of from 25 to 30 tons burthen, for at least one-half of all common years, and to vessels of much greater burthen a part of that time. From my peculiar circumstances, it is probable that for the last twelve months I have given as particular attention to the stage of the water in this river, as any other person in the country. In the month of March, 1831, in company with others, I commenced the building of a flatboat on the Sangamo, and finished and took her out in the course of the spring. Since that time, I have been concerned in the mill at New Salem. These circumstances are sufficient evidence, that I have not been very inattentive to the stages of the water. The time at which we crossed the mill dam, being in the last days of April, the water was lower than it had been since the breaking of winter in February, or than it was for several weeks after. The principal difficulties we encountered in descending the river, were from the drifted timber, which obstructions all know is not difficult to be removed. Knowing almost precisely the height of water at that time, I believe I am safe in saying that it has as often been higher as lower since.

From this view of the subject, it appears that my calculations with regard to the navigation of the Sangamo, cannot be unfounded in reason; but whatever may be its natural advantages, certain it is, that it never can be practically useful to any great extent, without being greatly improved by art. The drifted timber, as I have before mentioned, is the most formidable barrier to this object. Of all parts of this river, none will require so much labor in proportion, to make it navigable, as the last thirty or thirty-five miles; and going with the meanderings of the channel, when we are this distance above its mouth, we are only between twelve and eighteen miles above Beardstown, in something near a straight direction; and this route is upon such low ground as to retain water in many places during the season, and in all parts such as to draw two-thirds or three-fourths of the river water at all high stages.

This route is upon prairie land the whole distance; so that it appears to me, by removing the turf a sufficient width and damming up the old channel, the whole river in a short time would wash its way through, thereby curtailing the distance, and increasing the velocity of the current very considerably, while there would be no timber upon the banks to obstruct its navigation in the future; and being nearly straight, the timber which might float in at the head, would be apt to go clear through. There are also many places above this where the river, in its zigzag course, forms such complete peninsulas, as to be easier cut through at the necks than to remove the obstructions from the bends - which if done, would also lessen the distance.

What the cost of this work would be, I am unable to say. It is probable, however, it would not be greater than is common to streams of the same length. Finally, I believe the improvement of the Sangamo River, to be vastly important and highly desirable to the people of this county; and if elected, any measure in the legislature having this for its object, which may appear judicious, will meet my approbation, and shall receive my support.

Upon the subject of education, not presuming to dictate any plan or system respecting it, I can only say that I view it as the most important subject which we as a people can be engaged in. That every man may receive at least, a moderate education, and thereby be enabled to read the histories of his own and other countries, by which he may duly appreciate the value of our free institutions, appears to be an object of vital importance, even on this account alone, to say nothing of the advantages and satisfaction to be derived from all being able to read the scriptures and other works, both of a religious and moral nature, for themselves. For my part, I desire to see the time when education, and by its means, morality, sobriety, enterprise and industry, shall become much more general than at present, and should be gratified to have it in my power to contribute something to the advancement of any measure which might have a tendency to accelerate the happy period.

But, fellow citizens, I shall conclude. Considering the great degree of modesty which should always attend youth, it is probable I have already been more presuming than becomes me. However, upon the subjects of which I have treated, I have spoken as I thought. I may be wrong in regard to any or all of them; but holding it a sound maxim, that it is better to be only sometimes right, than at all times wrong, so soon as I discover my opinions to be erroneous, I shall be ready to renounce them.

Every man is said to have his peculiar ambition. Whether it be true or not, I can say for one that I have no other so great as that of being truly esteemed of my fellow men, by rendering myself worthy of their esteem. How far I shall succeed in gratifying this ambition, is yet to be developed. I am young and unknown to many of you. I was born and have ever remained in the most humble walks of life. I have no wealthy or popular relations to recommend me. My case is thrown exclusively upon the independent voters of this county, and if elected they will have conferred a favor upon me, for which I shall be unremitting in my labors to compensate. But if the good people in their wisdom shall see fit to keep me in the background, I have been too familiar with disappointments to be very much chagrined. Your friend and fellow citizen,

New Salem, March 9, 1832.
A. Lincoln

"The Perpetuation of Our Political Institutions" – Address to the Young Men's Lyceum of Springfield, Illinois, January 27, 1838

As a subject for the remarks of the evening, the perpetuation of our political institutions, is selected.

In the great journal of things happening under the sun, we, the American People, find our account running, under date of the nineteenth century of the Christian era. We find ourselves in the peaceful possession, of the fairest portion of the earth, as regards extent of territory, fertility of soil, and salubrity of climate. We find ourselves under the government of a system of political institutions, conducing more essentially to the ends of civil and religious liberty, than any of which the history of former times tells us. We, when mounting the stage of existence, found ourselves the legal inheritors of these fundamental blessings. We toiled not in the acquirement or establishment of them—they are a legacy bequeathed us, by a once hardy, brave, and patriotic, but now lamented and departed race of ancestors. Theirs was the task (and nobly they performed it) to possess themselves, and through themselves, us, of this goodly land; and to uprear upon its hills and its valleys, a political edifice of liberty and equal rights; 'tis ours only, to transmit these, the former, unprofaned by the foot of an invader; the latter, undecayed by the lapse of time, and untorn by usurpation—to the latest generation that fate shall permit the world to know. This task of gratitude to our fathers, justice to ourselves, duty to posterity, and love for our species in general, all imperatively require us faithfully to perform.

How, then, shall we perform it? At what point shall we expect the approach of danger? By what means shall we fortify against it? Shall we expect some transatlantic military giant, to step the Ocean, and crush us at a blow? Never! All the armies of Europe, Asia and Africa combined, with all the treasure of the earth (our own excepted) in their military chest; with a Buonaparte for a commander, could not by force, take a drink from the Ohio, or make a track on the Blue Ridge, in a Trial of a thousand years.

At what point then is the approach of danger to be expected? I answer, if it ever reach us, it must spring up amongst us. It cannot come from abroad. If destruction be our lot, we must ourselves be its author and finisher. As a nation of freemen, we must live through all time, or die by suicide.

I hope I am over wary; but if I am not, there is, even now, something of ill-omen amongst us. I mean the increasing disregard for law which pervades the country; the growing disposition to substitute the wild and furious passions, in lieu of the sober judgement of Courts; and the worse than savage mobs, for the executive ministers of justice. This disposition is awfully fearful in any community; and that it now exists in ours, though grating to our feelings to admit, it would be a violation of truth, and an insult to our intelligence, to deny. Accounts of outrages committed by mobs, form the every-day news of the times. They have pervaded the country, from New England to Louisiana;—they are neither peculiar to the eternal snows of the former, nor the burning suns of the latter;—they are not the creature of climate—neither are they confined to the slaveholding, or the non-slaveholding States. Alike, they spring up among the pleasure hunting masters of Southern slaves, and the order loving citizens of the land of steady habits. Whatever, then, their cause may be, it is common to the whole country.

It would be tedious, as well as useless, to recount the horrors of all of them. Those happening in the State of Mississippi, and at St. Louis, are, perhaps, the most dangerous in example, and revolting to humanity. In the Mississippi case, they first commenced by hanging the regular gamblers: a set of men, certainly not following for a livelihood, a very useful, or very honest occupation; but one which, so far from being forbidden by the laws, was actually licensed by an act of the Legislature, passed but a single year before. Next, negroes, suspected of conspiring to raise an insurrection, were caught up and hanged in all parts of the State: then, white men, supposed to be leagued with the negroes; and finally, strangers, from neighboring States, going thither on business, were, in many instances, subjected to the same fate. Thus went on this process of hanging, from gamblers to negroes, from negroes to white citizens, and from these to strangers; till, dead men were seen literally dangling from the boughs of trees upon every road side; and in numbers almost sufficient, to rival the native Spanish moss of the country, as a drapery of the forest.

Turn, then, to that horror-striking scene at St. Louis. A single victim was only sacrificed there. His story is very short; and is, perhaps, the most highly tragic, of any thing of its length, that has ever been witnessed in real life. A mulatto man, by the name of McIntosh, was seized in the street, dragged to the suburbs of the city, chained to a tree, and actually burned to death; and all within a single hour from the time he had been a freeman, attending to his own business, and at peace with the world.

Such are the effects of mob law; and such are the scenes, becoming more and more frequent in this land so lately famed for love of law and order; and the stories of which, have even now grown too familiar, to attract any thing more, than an idle remark.

But you are, perhaps, ready to ask, "What has this to do with the perpetuation of our political institutions?" I answer, it has much to do with it. Its direct consequences are, comparatively speaking, but a small evil; and much of its danger consists, in the proneness of our minds, to regard its direct, as its only consequences. Abstractly considered, the hanging of the gamblers at Vicksburg, was of but little consequence. They constitute a portion of population, that is worse than useless in any community; and their death, if no pernicious example be set by it, is never matter of reasonable regret with any one. If they were annually swept, from the stage of existence, by the plague or small pox, honest men would, perhaps, be much profited, by the operation. Similar too, is the correct reasoning, in regard to the burning of the negro at St. Louis. He had forfeited his life, by the perpetration of an outrageous murder, upon one of the most worthy and respectable citizens of the city; and had he not died as he did, he must have died by the sentence of the law, in a very short time afterwards. As to him alone, it was as well the way it was, as it could otherwise have been. But the example in either case, was fearful. When men take it in their heads to day, to hang gamblers, or burn murderers, they should recollect, that, in the confusion usually attending such transactions, they will be as likely to hang or burn some one, who is neither a gambler nor a murderer as one who is; and that, acting upon the example they set, the mob of to-morrow, may, and probably will, hang or burn some of them, by the very same mistake. And not only so; the innocent, those who have ever set their faces against violations of law in every shape, alike with the guilty, fall victims to the ravages of mob law; and thus it goes on, step by step, till all the walls erected for the defence of the persons and property of individuals, are trodden down, and disregarded. But all this even, is not the full extent of the evil. By such examples, by instances of the perpetrators of such acts going unpunished, the lawless in spirit, are encouraged to become lawless in practice; and having been used to no restraint, but dread of punishment, they thus become, absolutely unrestrained. Having ever regarded Government as their deadliest bane, they make a jubilee of the suspension of its operations; and pray for nothing so much, as its total annihilation. While, on the other hand, good men, men who love tranquility, who desire to abide by the laws, and enjoy their benefits, who would gladly spill their blood in the defence of their country; seeing their property destroyed; their families insulted, and their lives endangered; their persons injured; and seeing nothing in prospect that forebodes a change for the better; become tired of, and disgusted with, a Government that offers them no protection; and are not much averse to a change in which they imagine they have nothing to lose. Thus, then, by the operation of this mobocratic spirit, which all must admit, is now abroad in the land, the strongest bulwark of any Government, and particularly of those constituted like ours, may effectually be broken down and destroyed—I mean the attachment of the People.

Whenever this effect shall be produced among us; whenever the vicious portion of population shall be permitted to gather in bands of hundreds and thousands, and burn churches, ravage and rob provision stores, throw printing presses into rivers, shoot editors, and hang and burn obnoxious persons at pleasure, and with impunity; depend on it, this Government cannot last. By such things, the feelings of the best citizens will become more or less alienated from it; and thus it will be left without friends, or with too few, and those few too weak, to make their friendship effectual. At such a time and under such circumstances, men of sufficient talent and ambition will not be wanting to seize the opportunity, strike the blow, and overturn that fair fabric, which for the last half century, has been the fondest hope, of the lovers of freedom, throughout the world.

I know the American People are much attached to their Government;—I know they would suffer much for its sake;—I know they would endure evils long and patiently, before they would ever think of exchanging it for another. Yet, notwithstanding all this, if the laws be continually despised and disregarded, if their rights to be secure in their persons and property, are held by no better tenure than the caprice of a mob, the alienation of their affections from the Government is the natural consequence; and to that, sooner or later, it must come.

Here then, is one point at which danger may be expected.

The question recurs "how shall we fortify against it?" The answer is simple. Let every American, every lover of liberty, every well wisher to his posterity, swear by the blood of the Revolution, never to violate in the least particular, the laws of the country; and never to tolerate their violation by others. As the patriots of seventy-six did to the support of the Declaration of Independence, so to the support of the Constitution and Laws, let every American pledge his life, his property, and his sacred honor;—let every man remember that to violate the law, is to trample on the blood of his father, and to tear the character of his own, and his children's liberty. Let reverence for the laws, be breathed by every American mother, to the lisping babe, that prattles on her lap—let it be taught in schools, in seminaries, and in colleges;—let it be written in Primmers, spelling books, and in Almanacs;—let it be preached from the pulpit, proclaimed in legislative halls, and enforced in courts of justice. And, in short, let it become the political religion of the nation; and let the old and the young, the rich and the poor, the grave and the gay, of all sexes and tongues, and colors and conditions, sacrifice unceasingly upon its altars.

While ever a state of feeling, such as this, shall universally, or even, very generally prevail throughout the nation, vain will be every effort, and fruitless every attempt, to subvert our national freedom.

When I so pressingly urge a strict observance of all the laws, let me not be understood as saying there are no bad laws, nor that grievances may not arise, for the redress of which, no legal provisions have been made. I mean to say no such thing. But I do mean to say, that, although bad laws, if they exist, should be repealed as soon as possible, still while they continue in force, for the sake of example, they should be religiously observed. So also in unprovided cases. If such arise, let proper legal provisions be made for them with the least possible delay; but, till then, let them if not too intolerable, be borne with.

There is no grievance that is a fit object of redress by mob law. In any case that arises, as for instance, the promulgation of abolitionism, one of two positions is necessarily true; that is, the thing is right within itself, and therefore deserves the protection of all law and all good citizens; or, it is wrong, and therefore proper to be prohibited by legal enactments; and in neither case, is the interposition of mob law, either necessary, justifiable, or excusable.

But, it may be asked, why suppose danger to our political institutions? Have we not preserved them for more than fifty years? And why may we not for fifty times as long?

We hope there is no sufficient reason. We hope all dangers may be overcome; but to conclude that no danger may ever arise, would itself be extremely dangerous. There are now, and will hereafter be, many causes, dangerous in their tendency, which have not existed heretofore; and which are not too insignificant to merit attention. That our government should have been maintained in its original form from its establishment until now, is not much to be wondered at. It had many props to support it through that period, which now are decayed, and crumbled away. Through that period, it was felt by all, to be an undecided experiment; now, it is understood to be a successful one. Then, all that sought celebrity and fame, and distinction, expected to find them in the success of that experiment. Their all was staked upon it:—their destiny was inseparably linked with it. Their ambition aspired to display before an admiring world, a practical demonstration of the truth of a proposition, which had hitherto been considered, at best no better, than problematical; namely, the capability of a people to govern themselves. If they succeeded, they were to be immortalized; their names were to be transferred to counties and cities, and rivers and mountains; and to be revered and sung, and toasted through all time. If they failed, they were to be called knaves and fools, and fanatics for a fleeting hour; then to sink and be forgotten. They succeeded. The experiment is successful; and thousands have won their deathless names in making it so. But the game is caught; and I believe it is true, that with the catching, end the pleasures of the chase. This field of glory is harvested, and the crop is already appropriated. But new reapers will arise, and they, too, will seek a field. It is to deny, what the history of the world tells us is true, to suppose that men of ambition and talents will not continue to spring up amongst us. And, when they do, they will as naturally seek the gratification of their ruling passion, as others have so done before them. The question then, is, can that gratification be found in supporting and maintaining an edifice that has been erected by others? Most certainly it cannot. Many great and good men sufficiently qualified for any task they should undertake, may ever be found, whose ambition would aspire to nothing beyond a seat in Congress, a gubernatorial or a presidential chair; but such belong not to the family of the lion, or the tribe of the eagle. What! think you these places would satisfy an Alexander, a Caesar, or a Napoleon? Never! Towering genius disdains a beaten path. It seeks regions hitherto unexplored. It sees no distinction in adding story to story, upon the monuments of fame, erected to the memory of others. It denies that it is glory enough to serve under any chief. It scorns to tread in the footsteps of any predecessor, however illustrious. It thirsts and burns for distinction; and, if possible, it will have it, whether at the expense of emancipating slaves, or enslaving freemen. Is it unreasonable then to expect, that some man possessed of the loftiest genius, coupled with ambition sufficient to push it to its utmost stretch, will at some time, spring up among us? And when such a one does, it will require the people to be united with each other, attached to the government and laws, and generally intelligent, to successfully frustrate his designs.

Distinction will be his paramount object; and although he would as willingly, perhaps more so, acquire it by doing good as harm; yet, that opportunity being past, and nothing left to be done in the way of building up, he would set boldly to the task of pulling down.

Here then, is a probable case, highly dangerous, and such a one as could not have well existed heretofore.

Another reason which once was; but which, to the same extent, is now no more, has done much in maintaining our institutions thus far. I mean the powerful influence which the interesting scenes of the revolution had upon the passions of the people as distinguished from their judgment. By this influence, the jealousy, envy, and avarice, incident to our nature, and so common to a state of peace, prosperity, and conscious strength, were, for the time, in a great measure smothered and rendered inactive; while the deep rooted principles of hate, and the powerful motive of revenge, instead of being turned against each other, were directed exclusively against the British nation. And thus, from the force of circumstances, the basest principles of our nature, were either made to lie dormant, or to become the active agents in the advancement of the noblest of cause—that of establishing and maintaining civil and religious liberty.

But this state of feeling must fade, is fading, has faded, with the circumstances that produced it.

I do not mean to say, that the scenes of the revolution are now or ever will be entirely forgotten; but that like every thing else, they must fade upon the memory of the world, and grow more and more dim by the lapse of time. In history, we hope, they will be read of, and recounted, so long as the bible shall be read;—but even granting that they will, their influence cannot be what it heretofore has been. Even then, they cannot be so universally known, nor so vividly felt, as they were by the generation just gone to rest. At the close of that struggle, nearly every adult male had been a participator in some of its scenes. The consequence was, that of those scenes, in the form of a husband, a father, a son or a brother, a living history was to be found in every family—a history bearing the indubitable testimonies of its own authenticity, in the limbs mangled, in the scars of wounds received, in the midst of the very scenes related—a history, too, that could be read and understood alike by all, the wise and the ignorant, the learned and the unlearned. But those histories are gone.

They can be read no more forever. They were a fortress of strength; but, what invading foemen could never do, the silent artillery of time has done; the levelling of its walls. They are gone. They were a forest of giant oaks; but the all resistless hurricane has swept over them, and left only, here and there, a lonely trunk, despoiled of its verdure, shorn of its foliage; unshading and unshaded, to murmur in a few more gentle breezes, and to combat with its mutilated limbs, a few more ruder storms, then to sink, and be no more.

They were the pillars of the temple of liberty; and now, that they have crumbled away, that temple must fall, unless we, their descendants, supply their places with other pillars, hewn from the solid quarry of sober reason. Passion has helped us; but can do so no more. It will in future be our enemy. Reason, cold, calculating, unimpassioned reason, must furnish all the materials for our future support and defence. Let those materials be moulded into general intelligence, sound morality and, in particular, a reverence for the constitution and laws; and, that we improved to the last; that we remained free to the last; that we revered his name to the last; that, during his long sleep, we permitted no hostile foot to pass over or desecrate his resting place; shall be that which to learn the last trump shall awaken our WASHINGTON.

Upon these let the proud fabric of freedom rest, as the rock of its basis; and as truly as has been said of the only greater institution, "the gates of hell shall not prevail against it."

FIRST IMAGE OF ABRAHAM LINCOLN 1847

COURTSHIP

Among the more formidable challenges that confronted Lincoln in his new life was the prospect of courtship. Marriage in the mid-nineteenth century was, as now, prompted by mutual attraction and romance, but at the same time it was very often a practical, utilitarian agreement that served the ambitions of both parties. Lincoln was aware that his chances of social acceptance and political success would be improved by the right marriage, and his ambition was such that he sought out any advantage he might find to reach his goals.

Unfortunately, it was widely known that Lincoln was uncomfortable as a suitor. Most of what we know about Lincoln's romantic pursuits are the results of comments and recollections of Lincoln's contemporaries. Very little specific information is available in Lincoln's own words. There had been a brief "understanding" between Lincoln and Ann Rutledge, the daughter of one of New Salem's most prominent citizens, but the details of that relationship are not clear and there is some doubt that any relationship between the two existed at all. Lincoln's awkward relationship with Mary Owens, however, is well-documented. The two apparently met when a sister of Mary Owens decided to play matchmaker. Sometime in the autumn of 1836, she broached the subject to Lincoln who, intentionally or otherwise, gave her the impression that he was willing not only to court Mary Owens but to marry her as well. Mary Owens arrived in New Salem shortly thereafter and Lincoln felt obliged to follow through on his promise. But at the same time Lincoln was preparing to leave New Salem and move to Springfield where he was set to begin a new career as a lawyer. He was obviously having second thoughts about a relationship with Mary Owens, but was uncertain as to how he should handle the situation. His decision, as reflected in the following letters, reveals not only his feelings about Mary Owens, but his overall doubts and fears about courtship in general.

To Mary S. Owens, December 13, 1836

Vandalia, Decr. 13 1836

Mary

I have been sick ever since my arrival here, or I should have written sooner. It is but little difference, however, as I have verry little even yet to write. And more, the longer I can avoid the mortification of looking in the Post Office for your letter and not finding it, the better. You see I am mad about that old letter yet. I dont like verry well to risk you again. I'll try you once more any how.

The new State House is not yet finished, and consequently the legislature is doing little or nothing. The Governor delivered an inflamitory political Message, and it is expected there will be some sparring between the parties about [it as] soon as the two Houses get to business. Taylor [deliv]ered up his petitions for the New County to one of [our me]mbers this morning. I am told that he dispairs [of its] success on account of all the members from Morg[an C]ounty opposing it. There are names enough on the petitions[,] I think, to justify the members from our county in going for it; but if the members from Morgan oppose it, which they [say] they will, the chance will be bad.

Our chance to [take th]e seat of Government to Springfield is better than I ex-[pected]. An Internal Improvement Convention was held here since we met, which recommended a loan of several milli[ons] of dollars on the faith of the State to construct Rail Roads. Some of the legislature are for it[,] and some against it; which has the majority I can not tell. There is great strife and struggling for the office of U.S. Senator here at this time. It is probable we shall ease their pains in a few days. The opposition men have no candidate of their own, and consequently they smile as complacently at the angry snarls of the contending Van Buren candidates and their respective friends, as the christian does at Satan's rage. You recollect I mentioned in the outset of this letter that I had been unwell. That is the fact, though I believe I am about well now; but that, with other things I can not account for, have conspired and have gotten my spirits so low, that I feel that I would rather be any place in the world than here. I really can not endure the though of staying here ten weeks. Write back as soon as you get this, and if possible say something that will please me, for really I have not [been] pleased since I left you. This letter is so dry and [stupid] that I am ashamed to send it, but with my pres[ent feel]ings I can not do any better. Give my respects to M[r. and] Mrs. Abell and family. Your friend

LINCOLN
Miss Mary S. Owens

To Mary Owens, May 7, 1837

Friend Mary

I have commenced two letters to send you before this, both of which displeased me before I got half done, and so I tore them up. The first I thought wasn't serious enough, and the second was on the other extreme. I shall send this, turn out as it may.

This thing of living in Springfield is rather a dull business after all, at least it is so to me. I am quite as lonesome here as ever was anywhere in my life. I have been spoken to by but one woman since I have been here, and should not have been by her, if she could have avoided it. I've never been to church yet, nor probably shall not be soon. I stay away because I am concious I should not know how to behave myself-

I am often thinking about what we said of your coming to live at Springfield. I am afraid you would not be satisfied. There is a great deal of flourishing about in carriages here; which it would be your doom to see without sharing in it. You would have to be poor without the means of hiding your poverty. Do you believe you could bear that patiently? Whatever woman may cast her lot with mine should any ever do so, it is my intention to do all in my power to make her happy and contented; and there is nothing I can immagine, that would make me more unhappy than to fail in the effort. I know I should be much happier with you than the way I am, provided I saw no signs of discontent in you. What you have said to me may have been in jest, or I may have misunderstood it. If so, then let it be forgotten; if otherwise, I much wish you would think seriously before you decide. For my part I have already decided. What I have said I will most positively abide by, provided you wish it. My opinion is that you had better not do it. You have not been accustomed to hardship, and it may be more severe than you now immagine.

I know you are capable of thinking correctly on any subject, and if you deliberate maturely upon this, before you decide, then I am willing to abide your decision.

You must write me a good long letter after you get this. You have nothing else to do, and though it might not seem interesting to you, after you have written it, it would be a good deal of company to me in this "busy wilderness". Tell your sister I dont want to hear any more about selling out and moving. That gives me the hypo whenever I think of it.

Yours &c.
Lincoln

To Mary Owens, August 16, 1837

Springfield Aug. 16th 1837

Friend Mary

You will, no doubt, think it rather strange, that I should write you a letter on the same day on which we parted; and I can only account for it by supposing, that seeing you lately makes me think of you more than usual, while at our late meeting we had but few expressions of thoughts. You must know that I can not see you, or think of you, with entire indifference; and yet it may be, that you, are mistaken in regard to what my real feelings towards you are. If I knew you were not, I should not trouble you with this letter. Perhaps any other man would know enough without further information; but I consider it my peculiar right to plead ignorance, and your bounden duty to allow the plea. I want in all cases to do right, and most particularly so, in all cases with women. I want, at this particular time, more than any thing else, to do right with you, and if I knew it would be doing right, as I rather suspect it would, to let you alone, I would do it. And for the purpose of making the matter as plain as possible, I now say, that you can now drop the subject, dismiss your thoughts (if you ever had any) from me forever, and leave this letter unanswered, without calling forth one accusing murmer from me. And I will even go further, and say, that if it will add any thing to your comfort, or peace of mind, to do so, it is my sincere wish that you should. Do not understand by this, that I wish to cut your acquaintance. I mean no such thing. What I do wish is, that our further acquaintance shall depend upon yourself. If such further acquaintance would contribute nothing to your happiness, I am sure it would not to mine. If you feel yourself in any degree bound to me, I am now willing to release you, provided you wish it; while, on the other hand, I am willing, and even anxious to bind you faster, if I can be convinced that it will, in any considerable degree, add to your happiness. This, indeed, is the whole question with me. Nothing would make me more miserable than to believe you miserable---nothing more happy, than to know you were so.

In what I have now said, I think I can not be misunderstood; and to make myself understood, is the only object of this letter.

If it suits you best to not answer this---farewell---a long life and a merry one attend you. But if you conclude to write back, speak as plainly as I do. There can be neither harm nor danger, in saying, to me, any thing you think, just in the manner you think it.

My respects to your sister. Your friend LINCOLN.

Letter to Mrs. Orville Browning, April 1, 1838

Springfield, April 1, 1838.

Dear Madam: —

Without apologizing for being egotistical, I shall make the history of so much of my life as has elapsed since I saw you the subject of this letter. And, by the way, I now discover that, in order to give a full and intelligible account of the things I have done and suffered since I saw you, I shall necessarily have to relate some that happened before.

It was, then, in the autumn of 1836 that a married lady of my acquaintance and who was a great friend of mine, being about to pay a visit to her father and other relatives residing in Kentucky, proposed to me that on her return she would bring a sister of hers with her on condition that I would engage to become her brother-in-law with all convenient despatch. I, of course, accepted the proposal, for you know I could not have done otherwise, had I really been averse to it; but privately, between you and me I was most confoundedly well pleased with the project. I had seen the said sister some three years before, thought her intelligent and agreeable, and I saw no good objection to plodding life through hand in hand with her.

Time passed on, the lady took her journey, and in due time returned, sister in company sure enough. This stomached* me a little; for it appeared to me that her coming so readily showed that she was a trifle too willing; but, on reflection, it occurred to me that she might have been prevailed on by her married sister to come, without anything concerning me ever having been mentioned to her; and so I concluded that, if no other objection presented itself, I would consent to waive this. All this occurred to me on hearing of her arrival in the neighborhood; for, be it remembered, I had not yet seen her, except about three years previous, as above mentioned. In a few days we had an interview; and, although I had seen her before, she did not look as my imagination had pictured her. I knew she was over- size, but she now appeared a fair match for Falstaff. I knew she was called an "old maid," and I felt no doubt of the truth of at least half of the appellation ; but now, when I beheld her, I could not for my life avoid thinking of my mother ; and this, not from withered features, for her skin was too full of fat to permit of its contracting into wrinkles, but from her want of teeth, weather-beaten appearance in general, and from a kind of notion that ran in my head that nothing could have commenced at the size of infancy and reached her present bulk in less than thirty-five or forty years ; and, in short, I was not at all pleased with her. But what could I do? I had told her sister I would take her for better or for worse; and I made a point of honor and conscience in all things to stick to my word, especially if others had been induced to act on it, which in this case I had no doubt they had; for I was now fairly convinced that no other man on earth would have her, and hence the conclusion that they were bent on holding me to my bargain. "Well," thought I, "I have said it, and, be the consequences what they may, it shall not be my fault if I fail to do it." At once I determined to consider her my wife; and, this done, all my powers of discovery were put to work in search of perfections in her which might be fairly set off against her defects. I tried to imagine her handsome, which, but for her unfortunate corpulency, was actually true. Exclusive of this, no woman that I have ever seen has a finer face. I also tried to convince myself that the mind was much more to be valued than the person; and in this she was not inferior, as I could discover, to any with whom I had been acquainted.

Shortly after this, without coming to any positive under- standing with her, I set out for Vandalia, when and where you first saw me. During my stay there I had letters from her which did not change my opinion of either her intellect or intention, but on the contrary confirmed it in both.

All this while, although I was fixed, "firm as the surge- repelling rock," in my resolution, I found I was continually repenting the rashness which had led me to make it. Through life, I have been in no bondage, either real or imaginary, from the thralldom of which I so much desired to be free. After my return home, I saw nothing to change my opinion of her in any particular. She was the same, and so was I. I now spent my time in planning how I might get along through life after my contemplated change of circumstances should have taken place, and how I might procrastinate the evil day for a time, which I really dreaded as much, perhaps more, than an Irishman does the halter.

After all my suffering upon this deeply interesting subject, here I am, wholly, unexpectedly, completely, out of the "scrape"; and now I want to know if you can guess how I got out of it — out, clear, in every sense of the term ; no violation of word, honor, or conscience. I don't believe you can guess, and so I might as well tell you at once. As the lawyer says, it was done in the manner following, to-wit: After I had delayed the matter as long as I thought I could in honor do (which, by the way, had brought me round into the last fall), I concluded I might as well bring it to a consummation without further delay; and so I mustered my resolution, and made the proposal to her direct; but, shocking to relate, she answered. No. At first I supposed she did it through an affectation of modesty, which I thought but ill became her under the peculiar circumstances of her case; but on my renewal of the charge, I found she repelled it with greater firmness than before. I tried it again and again, but with the same success, or rather with the same want of success.

I finally was forced to give it up; at which I very unexpectedly found myself mortified almost beyond endurance. I was mortified, it seemed to me, in a hundred different ways. My vanity was deeply wounded by the reflection that I had been too stupid to discover her intentions, and at the same time never doubting that I understood them perfectly; and also that she, whom I had taught myself to believe nobody else would have, had actually rejected me with all my fancied greatness. And, to cap the whole, I then for the first time began to suspect that I was really a little in love with her. But let it all go. I'll try and outlive it. Others have been made fools of by the girls; but this can never with truth be said of me. I most emphatically, in this instance, made a fool of myself. I have now come to the conclusion never again to think of marrying, and for this reason: I can never be satisfied with any one who would be blockhead enough to have me.

When you receive this, write me a long yarn about something to amuse me. Give my respects to Mr. Browning.

Your sincere friend,
A. Lincoln.
Mrs. O. H. Browning.

MELANCHOLY

By the end of 1840, Lincoln had been a resident of Springfield, Illinois for almost four years. He had achieved some success as a young attorney, in part because of his partnership with an established attorney, John Todd Stuart. Lincoln was also a respected member of the state legislature and had made a reputation as a clever and effective politician. He had gained several close acquaintances and even overcome his fears of courtship to become engaged to one of the town's most eligible young ladies, Mary Todd. But it was all about to fall apart, at least from Lincoln's perspective. Stuart decided to dissolve their partnership so he could focus on political office. Although Lincoln had just been re-elected to a fourth term in the legislature, it had been a narrow victory and Lincoln was dubious about his prospects for winning the seat again. Among Lincoln's friends and acquaintances, there was only one person that could truly be called a close friend, and that was Joshua Speed. The two had met on the day Lincoln arrived in Springfield and—despite their markedly different backgrounds—formed a strong bond almost immediately. But now, as Lincoln confronted his sudden reversal of fortune, Speed announced that he had decided to return to his home in Kentucky. Lincoln's fears and insecurities now took control and, uncertain that he could be a suitable husband to Mary Todd, he suddenly broke off their engagement. Lincoln became morose, uncommunicative, and ignored most of his responsibilities in the legislature. At the end of January he had begun to recover somewhat, but when he wrote to his old law partner, John Todd Stuart, his depression was still clearly evident. The exact nature of that depression is impossible to diagnose from a distance of more than 150 years. But there is no doubt that Lincoln suffered frequently from spells of what was sometimes described as "melancholy." At times his disengagement from the world around him was brief and barely noticeable, but at other times it was pronounced enough to cause concern among his neighbors and colleagues. On at least two occasions, Lincoln's depression was so deep and intense that his friends became fearful for his safety. The early months of 1841 were one of those two occasions. A year later, however, Lincoln's situation had begun to improve. He formed a new law partnership with Stephen Logan and found the time to travel to Kentucky and visit with his old friend Speed, who was about to become engaged to be married. Upon his return, Lincoln wrote a series of letters to Speed that are remarkable for their emotion and familiarity. Nowhere else do we see Lincoln as an intimate friend and confidante; indeed, his friendship with Speed stands alone as the one known instance in Lincoln's life when he freely shared his deepest emotions.

To John T. Stuart, January 20, 1841

Springfield, Jany. 20th. 1841

Dear Stuart:

I have had no letter from you since you left. No matter for that. What I wish now is to speak of our Post-Office. You know I desired Dr. Henry to have that place when you left; I now desire it more than ever. I have, within the last few days, been making a most discreditable exhibition of myself in the way of hypochondriaism and thereby got an impression that Dr. Henry is necessary to my existence. Unless he gets that place he leaves Springfield. You therefore see how much I am interested in the matter.

We shall shortly forward you a petition in his favour signed by all or nearly all the Whig members of the Legislature, as well as other whigs.

This, together with what you know of the Dr.'s position and merits I sincerely hope will secure him the appointment. My heart is verry much set upon it.

Pardon me for not writing more; I have not sufficient composure to write a long letter. As ever yours

A. LINCOLN

From *Collected Works*. Abraham Lincoln Association, Springfield, IL. Roy P. Basler, editor; Marion Dolores Pratt and Lloyd A. Dunlap, assistant editors. Lincoln, Abraham, 1809-1865. New Brunswick, N.J.: Rutgers University Press, 1953. Copyright © The Abraham Lincoln Association. Reprinted by permission.

To John T. Stuart, January 23, 1841

Jany. 23rd. 1841- Springfield, Ills.

Dear Stuart:

Yours of the 3rd. Inst. is recd. & I proceed to answer it as well as I can, tho' from the deplorable state of my mind at this time, I fear I shall give you but little satisfaction. About the matter of the congressional election, I can only tell you, that there is a bill now before the Senate adopting the General Ticket system; but whether the party have fully determined on it's adoption is yet uncertain. There is no sign of opposition to you among our friends, and none that I can learn among our enemies; tho', of course, there will be, if the Genl. Ticket be adopted. The Chicago American, Peoria Register, & Sangamo Journal, have already hoisted your flag upon their own responsibility; & the other whig papers of the District are expected to follow immediately. On last evening there was a meeting of our friends at Butler's; and I submitted the question to them & found them unanamously in favour of having you announced as a candidate. A few of us this morning, however, concluded, that as you were already being announced in the papers, we would delay announcing you, as by your own authority for a week or two. We thought that to appear too keen about it might spur our opponents on about their Genl. Ticket project. Upon the whole, I think I may say with certainty, that your reelection is sure, if it be in the power of the whigs to make it so.

For not giving you a general summary of news, you must pardon me; it is not in my power to do so. I am now the most miserable man living. If what I feel were equally distributed to the whole human family, there would not be one cheerful face on the earth. Whether I shall ever be better I can not tell; I awfully forebode I shall not. To remain as I am is impossible; I must die or be better, it appears to me. The matter you speak of on my account, you may attend to as you say, unless you shall hear of my condition forbidding it. I say this, because I fear I shall be unable to attend to any bussiness here, and a change of scene might help me. If I could be myself, I would rather remain at home with Judge Logan. I can write no more. Your friend, as ever---
A. Lincoln

From *Collected Works*. Abraham Lincoln Association, Springfield, IL. Roy P. Basler, editor; Marion Dolores Pratt and Lloyd A. Dunlap, assistant editors. Lincoln, Abraham, 1809-1865. New Brunswick, N.J.: Rutgers University Press, 1953. Copyright © The Abraham Lincoln Association. Reprinted by permission.

To Joshua F. Speed, January 3 [?], 1842

January 3 [?], 1842

My Dear Speed:

Feeling, as you know I do, the deepest solicitude for the success of the enterprize you are engaged in, I adopt this as the last method I can invent to aid you, in case (which God forbid) you shall need any aid. I do not place what I am going to say on paper, because I can say it any better in that way than I could by word of mouth; but because, were I to say it orrally, before we part, most likely you would forget it at the verry time when it might do you some good. As I think it reasonable that you will feel verry badly some time between this and the final consummation of your purpose, it is intended that you shall read this just at such a time.

Why I say it is reasonable that you will feel verry badly yet, is, because of three special causes, added to the general one which I shall mention.

The general cause is, that you are naturally of a nervous temperament; and this I say from what I have seen of you personally, and what you have told me concerning your mother at various times, and concerning your brother William at the time his wife died.

The first special cause is, your exposure to bad weather on your journey, which my experience clearly proves to be verry severe on defective nerves.

The second is, the absence of all business and conversation of friends, which might divert your mind, and give it occasional rest from that intensity of thought, which will some times wear the sweetest idea thread-bare and turn it to the bitterness of death.

The third is, the rapid and near approach of that crisis on which all your thoughts and feelings concentrate.

If from all these causes you shall escape and go through triumphantly, without another "twinge of the soul," I shall be most happily, but most egregiously deceived.

If, on the contrary, you shall, as I expect you will at some time, be agonized and distressed, let me, who have some reason to speak with judgement on such a subject, beseech you, to ascribe it to the causes I have mentioned; and not to some false and ruinous suggestion of the Devil.

"But" you will say "do not your causes apply to every one engaged in a like undertaking?"

By no means. The particular causes, to a greater or less extent, perhaps do apply in all cases; but the general one, nervous debility, which is the key and conductor of all the particular ones, and without which they would be utterly harmless, though it does pertain to you, does not pertain to one in a thousand. It is out of this, that the painful difference between you and the mass of the world springs.

I know what the painful point with you is, at all times when you are unhappy. It is an apprehension that you do not love her as you should. What nonsense!---How came you to court her? Was it because you thought she desired it; and that you had given her reason to expect it? If it was for that, why did not the same reason make you court Ann Todd, and at least twenty others of whom you can think, & to whom it would apply with greater force than to her? Did you court her for her wealth? Why, you knew she had none. But you say you reasoned yourself into it. What do you mean by that? Was it not, that you found yourself unable to reason yourself out of it? Did you not think, and partly form the purpose, of courting her the first time you ever saw or heard of her? What had reason to do with it, at that early stage? There was nothing at that time for reason to work upon. Whether she was moral, aimiable, sensible, or even of good character, you did not, nor could not then know; except perhaps you might infer the last from the company you found her in. All you then did or could know of her, was her personal appearance and deportment; and these, if they impress at all, impress the heart and not the head.

Say candidly, were not those heavenly black eyes, the whole basis of all your easily reasoning on the subject?

After you and I had once been at her residence, did you not go and take me all the way to Lexington and back, for no other purpose but to get to see her again, on our return, [in that] seeming to take a trip for that express object?

What earthly consideration would you take to find her scouting and despising you, and giving herself up to another? But of this you have no apprehension; and therefore you can not bring it home to your feelings.

I shall be so anxious about you, that I want you to write me every mail. Your friend

LINCOLN

To Joshua F. Speed, February 3, 1842

Springfield, Ills. Feby. 3- 1842-

Dear Speed:

Your letter of the 25th. Jany. came to hand to-day. You well know that I do not feel my own sorrows much more keenly than I do yours, when I know of them; and yet I assure you I was not much hurt by what you wrote me of your excessively bad feeling at the time you wrote. Not that I am less capable of sympathising with you now than ever; not that I am less your friend than ever, but because I hope and believe, that your present anxiety and distress about her health and her life, must and will forever banish those horid doubts, which I know you sometimes felt, as to the truth of your affection for her. If they can be once and forever removed, (and I almost feel a presentiment that the Almighty has sent your present affliction expressly for that object) surely, nothing can come in their stead, to fill their immeasurable measure of misery. The death scenes of those we love, are surely painful enough; but these we are prepared to, and expect to see. They happen to all, and all know they must happen. Painful as they are, they are not an unlooked-for-sorrow. Should she, as you fear, be destined to an early grave, it is indeed, a great consolation to know that she is so well prepared to meet it. Her religion, which you once disliked so much, I will venture you now prize most highly.

But I hope your melancholly bodings as to her early death, are not well founded. I even hope, that ere this reaches you, she will have returned with improved and still improving health; and that you will have met her, and forgotten the sorrows of the past, in the enjoyment of the present.

I would say more if I could; but it seems I have said enough. It really appears to me that you yourself ought to rejoice, and not sorrow, at this indubitable evidence of your undying affection for her. Why Speed, if you did not love her, although you might not wish her death, you would most calmly be resigned to it. Perhaps this point is no longer a question with you, and my pertenacious dwelling upon it, is a rude intrusion upon your feelings. If so, you must pardon me. You know the Hell I have suffered on that point, and how tender I am upon it. You know I do not mean wrong.

I have been quite clear of hypo since you left,---even better than I was along in the fall.

I have seen Sarah but once. She seemed verry cheerful, and so, I said nothing to her about what we spoke of.

Old uncle Billy Herndon is dead; and it is said this evening that uncle Ben Ferguson will not live. This I believe is all the news, and enough at that unless it were better.

Write me immediately on the receipt of this. Your friend, as ever LINCOLN

To Joshua F. Speed [private], February 25, 1842

Springfield, Feb: 25- 1842-

Dear Speed:

I received yours of the 12th. written the day you went down to William's place, some days since; but delayed answering it, till I should receive the promised one, of the 16th., which came last night. I opened the latter, with intense anxiety and trepidation---so much, that although it turned out better than I expected, I have hardly yet, at the distance of ten hours, become calm.

I tell you, Speed, our forebodings, for which you and I are rather peculiar, are all the worst sort of nonsense. I fancied, from the time I received your letter of saturday, that the one of wednesday was never to come; and yet it did come, and what is more, it is perfectly clear, both from it's tone and handwriting, that you were much happier, or, if you think the term preferable, less miserable, when you wrote it, than when you wrote the last one before. You had so obviously improved, at the verry time I so much feared, you would have grown worse. You say that "something indescribably horrible and alarming still haunts you.["] You will not say that three months from now, I will venture. When your nerves once get steady now, the whole trouble will be over forever. Nor should you become impatient at their being even verry slow, in becoming steady. Again; you say you much fear that that Elysium of which you have dreamed so much, is never to be realized. Well, if it shall not, I dare swear, it will not be the fault of her who is now your wife. I now have no doubt that it is the peculiar misfortune of both you and me, to dream dreams of Elysium far exceeding all that any thing earthly can realize. Far short of your dreams as you may be, no woman could do more to realize them, than that same black eyed Fanny. If you could but contemplate her through my immagination, it would appear ridiculous to you, that any one should for a moment think of being unhappy with her. My old Father used to have a saying that "If you make a bad bargain, hug it the tighter"; and it occurs to me, that if the bargain you have just closed can possibly be called a bad one, it is certainly the most pleasant one for applying that maxim to, which my fancy can, by any effort, picture.

I write another letter enclosing this, which you can show her, if she desires it. I do this, because, she would think strangely perhaps should you tell her that you receive no letters from me; or, telling her you do, should refuse to let her see them.

I close this, entertaining the confident hope, that every successive letter I shall have from you, (which I here pray may not be few, nor far between,) may show you possessing a more steady hand, and cheerful heart, than the last preceding it. As ever, your friend
LINCOLN

To Joshua F. Speed, February 25, 1842

Springfield, Feby. 25- 1842-

Dear Speed:

Yours of the 16th. Inst. announcing that Miss Fanny and you "are no more twain, but one flesh," reached me this morning. I have no way of telling how much happiness I wish you both; tho' I believe you both can conceive it. I fell som[e] what jealous of both of you now; you will be so exclusively concerned for one another, that I shall be forgotten entirely. My acquaintance with Miss Fanny (I call her thus, lest you should think I am speaking of your mother) was too short for me to reasonably hope to long be remembered by her; and still, I am sure, I shall not forget her soon. Try if you can not remind her of that debt she owes me; and be sure you do not interfere to prevent her paying it.

I regret to learn that you have resolved to not return to Illinois. I shall be verry lonesome without you. How miserably things seem to be arranged in this world. If we have no friends, we have no pleasure; and if we have them, we are sure to lose them, and be doubly pained by the loss. I did hope she and you would make your home here; but I own I have no right to insist. You owe obligations to her, ten thousand times more sacred than any you can owe to others; and, in that light, let them be respected and observed. It is natural that she should desire to remain with her relatives and friends. As to friends, however, she could not need them any where; she would have them in abundance here.

Give my kind rememberance to Mr. Williamson and his family, particularly Miss Elizabeth --also to your Mother, brothers, and sisters. Ask little Eliza Davis if she will ride to town with me if I come there again.

And, finally, give Fanny a double reciprocation of all the love she sent me. Write me often, and believe me Yours forever

LINCOLN

P.S. Poor Eastham is gone at last. He died a while before day this morning. They say he was verry loth to die.
No clerk is appointed yet. L.

To Joshua F. Speed, March 27, 1842

Springfield, March 27th. 1842

Dear Speed:

Yours of the 10th. Inst. was received three or four days since. You know I am sincere, when I tell you, the pleasure it's contents gave me was and is inexpressible. As to your farm matter, I have no sympathy with you. I have no farm, nor ever expect to have; and, consequently, have not studied the subject enough to be much interested with it. I can only say that I am glad you are satisfied and pleased with it.

But on that other subject, to me of the most intense interest, whether in joy or sorrow, I never had the power to withhold my sympathy from you. It can not be told, how it now thrills me with joy, to hear you say you are "far happier than you ever expected to be." That much I know is enough. I know you too well to suppose your expectations were not, at least sometimes, extravagant; and if the reality exceeds them all, I say, enough, dear Lord. I am not going beyond the truth, when I tell you, that the short space it took me to read your last letter, gave me more pleasure, than the total sum of all I have enjoyed since that fatal first of Jany.'41. Since then, it seems to me, I should have been entirely happy, but for the never-absent idea, that there is one still unhappy whom I have contributed to make so. That still kills my soul. I can not but reproach myself, for even wishing to be happy while she is otherwise. She accompanied a large party on the Rail Road cars, to Jacksonville last monday; and on her return, spoke, so that I heard of it, of having enjoyed the trip exceedingly. God be praised for that.

You know with what sleepless vigilance I have watched you, ever since the commencement of your affair; and altho' I am now almost confident it is useless, I can not forbear once more to say that I think it is even yet possible for your spirits to flag down and leave you miserable. If they should, dont fail to remember that they can not long remain so.

One thing I can tell you which I know you will be glad to hear; and that is, that I have seen Sarah, and scrutinized her feelings as well as I could, and am fully convinced, she is far happier now, than she has been for the last fifteen months past.

You will see by the last Sangamo Journal that I made a Temperance speech on the 22. of Feb. which I claim that Fanny and you shall read as an act of charity to me; for I can not learn that any body else has read it, or is likely to. Fortunately, it is not very long and I shall deem it a sufficient compliance with my request, if one of you listens while the other reads it. As to your Lockridge matter, it is only necessary to say that there has been no court since you left, and that the next, commences to-morrow morning, during which I suppose we can not fail to get a judgement.

I wish you would learn of Everett what he will take, over and above a discharge for all trouble we have been at, to take his business out of our hands and give it to somebody else. It is impossible to collect money on that or any other claim here now; and altho' you know I am not a very petulant ma[n,] I declare I am almost out of patience with [Mr.] Everett's endless importunity. It seems like [he n]to only writes all the letters he can himself; b[ut] gets every body else in Louisville and vicinity to be constantly writing to us about his claim.

I have always [h]eard that Mr. Evere[tt is] a very clever fellow, and I am very [sorry] he can not be obliged; but it does seem to me he ought to know we are interested [to] collect his money, and therefore would do [it] if we could. I am neither joking nor in a [pet] when I say we would thank him to transfer h[is] business to some other, without any compensation for what we have done, provided he will see the court cost paid, for which we are security.

The sweet violet you enclosed, came safely to hand, but it was so dry, and mashed so fla[t,] that it crumbled to dust at the first attempt to handle it. The juice that mashed out of it, stained a [place] on the letter, which I mean to preserve and ch[erish] for the sake of her who procured it to be se[nt.] My renewed good wishes to her, in particula[r,] and generally to all such of your relatives as know me. As ever LINCOLN

JOSHUA SPEED WITH HIS WIFE FANNY.

McClure's Magazine 6:5 (April 1896), 435.

ACCOUNTABILITY

Lincoln's fourth and final term in the Illinois legislature came to a close in 1842, and Lincoln found himself casting about for some means to maintain his political relevance among his fellow Whig Party members. By this time he was an accomplished writer and had already written several anonymous letters to the local Whig newspaper attacking his political enemies, so it is not surprising that he turned to his pen in an attempt to wield influence. There had appeared previously in the local paper a series of letters from the fictitious "Lost Townships," in which the anonymous author—who signed the letters as "Aunt 'Becca"—poked fun at local Democratic politicians. Using this same device, Lincoln also wrote a letter to the paper, but Lincoln's sharp wit and blunt humor went well beyond anything that had appeared before. His main target was James Shields, the state bank auditor, who had recently announced that the state of Illinois would no longer accept notes from the state bank as payment. To Lincoln and other Whigs, such a decision was not motivated by economic necessity but instead by a desire to destroy the state bank, an ideological objective that Democrats such as Shields were known to favor. Lincoln's "Rebecca Letter" was masterfully written, relied heavily on the frontier vernacular with which he was so familiar, and shows yet another dimension to his writing style. Shields, however, was incensed at such a bold and blatant assault on his character and honor. He eventually discovered the identity of the author and promptly challenged Lincoln to a duel. The resulting fiasco, as recounted in the documents below, taught Lincoln a good deal about effective writing and represent a sort of turning point in his approach to writing. As Lincoln learned in the summer of 1842, ill-chosen words can have real consequences.

Letter from the Lost Townships [the "Rebecca Letter"], August 27, 1842

Lost Townships, Aug. 27, 1842.

Dear Mr. Printer:

I see you printed that long letter I sent you a spell ago ---I'm quite encouraged by it, and can't keep from writing again. I think the printing of my letters will be a good thing all round,---it will give me the benefit of being known by the world, and give the world the advantage of knowing what's going on in the Lost Townships, and give your paper respectability besides. So here come another. Yesterday afternoon I hurried through cleaning up the dinner dishes, and stepped over to neighbor S--- to see if his wife Peggy was as well as mought be expected, and hear what they called the baby. Well, when I got there, and just turned round the corner of his log cabin, there he was setting on the door-step reading a newspaper.

'How are you Jeff,' says I,---he sorter started when he heard me, for he hadn't seen me before. 'Why,' says he, 'I'm mad as the devil, aunt Becca.'

'What about,' says I, 'aint its hair the right color? None of that nonsense, Jeff---there aint an honester woman in the Lost Township than---'

'Than who?' says he, 'what the mischief are you about?'

I began to see I was running the wrong trail, and so says I, 'O nothing, I guess I was mistaken a little, that's all. But what is it you're mad about?'

'Why,' says he, 'I've been tugging ever since harvest getting out wheat and hauling it to the river, to raise State Bank paper enough to pay my tax this year, and a little school debt I owe; and now just as I've got it, here I open this infernal Extra Register, expecting to find it full of "glorious democratic victories," and "High Comb'd Cocks," when, lo and behold, I find a set of fellows calling themselves officers of State, have forbidden the tax collectors and school commissioners to receive State paper at all; and so here it is, dead on my hands. I don't now believe all the plunder I've got will fetch ready cash enough to pay my taxes and that school debt.'

I was a good deal thunderstruck myself; for that was the first I had heard of the proclamation, and my old man was pretty much in the same fix with Jeff. We both stood a moment, staring at one another without knowing what to say. At last says I, 'Mr. S--- let me look at that paper.' He handed it to me, when I read the proclamation over.

'There now,' says he, 'did you ever see such a piece of impudence and imposition as that?' I saw Jeff was in a good tune for saying some ill-natured things, and so I tho't I would just argue a little on the contrary side, and make him rant a spell if I could.

'Why,' says I, looking as dignified and thoughtful as I could, 'it seems pretty tough to be sure, to have to raise silver where there's none to be raised; but then you see "there will be danger of loss" if it aint done.'

'Loss, damnation!' says he, 'I defy Daniel Webster, I defy King Solomon, I defy the world,---I defy---I defy---yes, I defy even you, aunt Becca, to show how the people can lose any thing by paying their taxes in State paper.' 'Well,' says I, 'you see what the officers of State say about it, and they are a desarnin set of men.' `But,' says I, `I guess you're mistaken about what the proclamation says; it don't say the people will lose any thing by the paper money being taken for taxes. It only says "there will be danger of loss," and though it is tolerable plain that the people can't lose by paying their taxes in something they can get easier than silver, instead of having to pay silver; and though it is just as plain, that the State can't lose by taking State Bank paper, however low it may be, while she owes the Bank more than the whole revenue, and can pay that paper over on her debt, dollar for dollar; still there is danger of loss to the "officers of State," and you know Jeff, we can't get along without officers of State.'

`Damn officers of State,' says he, `that's what you whigs are always hurraing for.' `Now don't swear so Jeff,' says I, `you know I belong to the meetin, and swearin hurts my feelins.' `Beg pardon, aunt Becca,' says he, `but I do say its enough to make Dr. Goddard swear, to have tax to pay in silver, for nothing only that Ford may get his two thousand a year, and Shields his twenty four hundred a year, and Carpenter his sixteen hundred a year, and all without "danger of loss" by taking it in State paper.' `Yes, yes, it's plain enough now what these officers of State mean by "danger of loss." Wash, I 'spose, actually lost fifteen hundred dollars out of the three thousand that two of these "officers of State" let him steal from the Treasury, by being compelled to take it in State paper. Wonder if we don't have a proclamation before long, commanding us to make up this loss to Wash in silver.'

And so he went on, till his breath run out, and he had to stop. I couldn't think of any thing to say just then: and so I begun to look over the paper again. `Aye! here's another proclamation, or something like it.' `Another!' says Jeff, `and whose egg is it, pray?' I looked to the bottom of it, and read aloud, `Your obedient servant, JAS SHIELDS, Auditor.'

`Aha!' says Jeff, `one of them same three fellows again. Well read it, and let's hear what of it.' I read on till I came to where it says, "The object of this measure is to suspend the collection of the revenue for the current year." `Now stop, now stop,' says he, `that's a lie aready, and I don't want to hear of it.' `O may be not,' says I.

`I say it---is---a---lie. --- Suspend the collection, indeed! Will the collectors that have taken their oaths to make the collection DARE to suspend it? Is there any thing in the law requiring them to perjure themselves at the bidding of Jas. Shields? Will the greedy gullet of the penitentiary be satisfied with swallowing him instead of all them if they should venture to obey him? And would he not discover some "danger of loss" and be off, about the time it came to taking their places?

'And suppose the people attempt to suspend by refusing to pay, what then? The collectors would just jerk up their horses, and cows, and the like, and sell them to the highest bidder for silver in hand, without valuation or redemption. Why, Shields didn't believe that story himself---it was never meant for the truth. If it was true, why was it not writ till five days after the proclamation? Why didn't Carlin and Carpenter sign it as well as Shields? Answer me that, aunt Becca. I say its a lie, and not a well told one at that. It grins out like a copper dollar. Shields is a fool as well as a liar. With him truth is out of the question, and as for getting a good bright passable lie out of him, you might as well try to strike fire from a cake of tallow. I stick to it, its all an infernal whig lie.'

'A whig lie,---Highty! Tighty!!'

'Yes, a whig lie; and its just like every thing the cursed British whigs do. First they'll do some devilment, and then they'll tell a lie to hide it. And they don't care how plain a lie it is; they think they can cram any sort of a one down the throats of the ignorant loco focos, as they call the democrats.'

'Why, Jeff, you're crazy---you don't mean to say Shields is a whig.'

'Yes I do.'

'Why, look here, the proclamation is in your own democratic paper as you call it.'

'I know it, and what of that? They only printed it to let us democrats see the deviltry the whigs are at.'

'Well, but Shields is the Auditor of this loco---I mean this democratic State.'

'So he is, and Tyler appointed him to office.'

'Tyler appointed him?'

'Yes (if you must chaw it over) Tyler appointed him, or if it wasn't him it was old granny Harrison, and that's all one. I tell you, aunt Becca, there's no mistake about his being a whig---why his very looks shows it---every thing about him shows it---if I was deaf and blind I could tell him by the smell. I seed him when I was down in Springfield last winter. They had a sort of a gatherin there one night, among the grandees, they called a fair. All the galls about town was there, and all the handsome widows, and married women, finickin about, trying to look like galls, tied as tight in the middle, and puffed out at both ends like bundles of fodder that hadn't been stacked yet, but wanted stackin pretty bad. And then they had tables all round the house kivered over with baby caps, and pin-cushions, and ten thousand such little nicknacks, tryin to sell 'em to the fellows that were bowin and scrapin, and kungeerin about 'em. They wouldn't let no democrats in, for fear they'd disgust the ladies, or scare the little galls, or dirty the floor. I looked in at the window, and there was this same fellow Shields floatin about on the air, without heft or earthly substance, just like a lock of cat-fur where cats had been fightin.

`He was paying his money to this one and that one, and tother one, and sufferin great loss because it wasn't silver instead of State paper; and the sweet distress he seemed to be in,---his very features, in the exstatic agony of his soul, spoke audibly and distinctly---"Dear girls, it is distressing, but I cannot marry you all. Too well I know how much you suffer; but do, do remember, it is not my fault that I am so handsome and so interesting."

`As this last was expressed by a most exquisite contortion of his face, he seized hold of one of their hands and squeezed, and held on to it about a quarter of an hour. O, my good fellow, says I to myself, if that was one of our democratic galls in the Lost Township, the way you'd get a brass pin let into you, would be about up to the head. He a democrat! Fiddle-sticks! I tell you, aunt Becca, he's a whig, and no mistake: nobody but a whig could make such a conceity dunce of himself.'

`Well,' says I, `may be he is, but if he is, I'm mistaken the worst sort.

`May be so; may be so; but if I am I'll suffer by it; I'll be a democrat if it turns out that Shields is a whig; considerin you shall be a whig if he turns out a democrat.'

`A bargain, by jingoes,' says he, `but how will we find out.'

`Why,' says I, `we'll just write and ax the printer.' `Agreed again,' says he, `and by thunder if it does turn out that Shields is a democrat, I never will ---'

`Jefferson,---Jefferson---'

`What do you want, Peggy.'

`Do get through your everlasting clatter some time, and bring me a gourd of water; the child's been crying for a drink this livelong hour.'

'Let it die then, it may as well die for water as to be taxed to death to fatten officers of State.'

Jeff run off to get the water though, just like he hadn't been sayin any thing spiteful; for he's a rall good hearted fellow, after all, once you get at the foundation of him.

I walked into the house, and 'why Peggy,' says I, 'I declare, we like to forgot you altogether.' 'O yes,' says she, 'when a body can't help themselves, every body soon forgets 'em; but thank God by day after to-morrow I shall be well enough to milk the cows and pen the calves, and wring the contrary one's tails for 'em, and no thanks to nobody.' 'Geod evening, Peggy,' says I, and so I sloped, for I seed she was mad at me, for making Jeff neglect her so long.

And now Mr. Printer, will you be sure to let us know in your next paper whether this Shields is a whig or a democrat? I don't care about it for myself, for I know well enough how it is already, but I want to convince Jeff. It may do some good to let him, and others like him, know who and what these officers of State are. It may help to send the present hypocritical set to where they belong, and to fill the places they now disgrace with men who will do more work, for less pay, and take a fewer airs while they are doing it. It aint sensible to think that the same men who get us into trouble will change their course; and yet its pretty plain, if some change for the better is not made, its not long that neither Peggy, or I, or any of us, will have a cow left to milk, or a calf's tail to wring. Yours, truly, REBECCA---.

To James Shields, September 17, 1842

Tremont, Sept. 17, 1842

Jas. Shields, Esq.

Your note of to-day was handed me by Gen. Whiteside. In that note you say you have been informed, through the medium of the editor of the Journal, that I am the author of certain articles in that paper which you deem personally abusive of you: and without stopping to enquire whether I really am the author, or to point out what is offensive in them, you demand an unqualified retraction of all that is offensive; and then proceed to hint at consequences.

Now, sir, there is in this so much assumption of facts, and so much of menace as to consequences, that I cannot submit to answer that note any farther than I have, and to add, that the consequence to which I suppose you allude, would be matter of as great regret to me as it possibly could to you.

Respectfully,
A. LINCOLN.

Memorandum of Duel Instructions to Elias H. Merryman, September 19, 1842

[September 19, 1842]

In case Whitesides shall signify a wish to adjust this affair without further difficulty, let him know that if the present papers be withdrawn, & a note from Mr. Shields asking to know if I am the author of the articles of which he complains, and asking that I shall make him gentlemanly satisfaction, if I am the author, and this without menace, or dictation as to what that satisfaction shall be, a pledge is made, that the following answer shall be given---

"I did write the `Lost Township' letter which appeared in the Journal of the 2nd. Inst. but had no participation, in any form, in any other article alluding to you. I wrote that, wholly for political effect. I had no intention of injuring your personal or private character or standing as a man or a gentleman; and I did not then think, and do not now think that that article, could produce or has produced that effect against you, and had I anticipated such an effect I would have forborne to write it. And I will add, that your conduct towards me, so far as I knew, had always been gentlemanly; and that I had no personal pique against you, and no cause for any."

If this should be done, I leave it with you to arrange what shall & what shall not be published.

If nothing like this is done---the preliminaries of the fight are to be---

1st. Weapons---Cavalry broad swords of the largest size, precisely equal in all respects---and such as now used by the cavalry company at Jacksonville.

2nd. Position---A plank ten feet long, & from nine to twelve inches broad to be firmly fixed on edge, on the ground, as the line between us which neither is to pass his foot over upon forfeit of his life. Next a line drawn on the ground on either side of said plank & paralel with it, each at the distance of the whole length of the sword and three feet additional from the plank; and the passing of his own such line by either party during the fight shall be deemed a surrender of the contest.

3. Time---On thursday evening at five o'clock if you can get it so; but in no case to be at a greater distance of time than friday evening at five o'clock.

4th. Place---Within three miles of Alton on the opposite side of the river, the particular spot to be agreed on by you.

Any preliminary details coming within the above rules, you are at liberty to make at your discretion; but you are in no case to swerve from these rules, or to pass beyond their limits.

To Joshua F. Speed, October 5, 1842

Springfield, Oct. 5 1842-

Dear Speed:

You have heard of my duel with Shields, and I have now to inform you that the duelling business still rages in this city. Day-before-yesterday Shields challenged Butler, who accepted, and proposed figh[t]ing next morning at sun-rising in Bob. Allen's meadow, one hundred yards distance with rifles. To this, Whitesides, Shields' second, said "No" because of the law. Thus ended, duel No. 2. Yesterday, Whitesides chose to consider himself insulted by Dr. Merryman, and so, sent him a kind of quasi challenge inviting him to meet him at the planter's House in St. Louis on the next friday to settle their difficulty. Merryman made me his friend, and sent W. a note enquiring to know if he meant his note as a challenge, and if so, that he would, according to the law in such case made and provided, prescribe the terms of the meeting. W. Returned for answer, that if M. would meet him at the Planter's House as desired, he would challenge him. M. replied in a note, that he denied W's right to dictate time and place; but that he, M, would would [sic] waive the question of time, and meet him at Louisiana Missouri. Upon my presenting this note to W. and stating verbally, it's contents, he declined receiving it, saying he had business at St. Louis, and it was as near as Louisiana. Merryman then directed me to notify Whitesides, that he should publish the correspondence between them with such comments as he thought fit. This I did. Thus it stood at bed time last night. This morning Whitesides, by his friend Shields, is praying for a new---trial, on the ground that he was mistaken in Merrymans proposition to meet him at Louisiana Missouri thinking it was the State of Louisiana. This Merryman hoots at, and is preparing his publication---while the town is in a ferment and a street fight somewhat anticipated.

But I began this letter not for what I have been writing; but to say something on that subject which you know to be of such infinite solicitude to me. The immense suffering you endured from the first days of September till middle of February you never tried to conceal from me, and I well understood. You have now been the husband of a lovely woman nearly eight months. That you are happier now than you were the day you married her I well know; for without, you would not be living. But I have your word for it too; and the returning elasticity of spirits which is manifested in your letters. But I want to ask a closer question---"Are you now, in feeling as well as judgement, glad you are married as you are?" From any body but me, this would be an impudent question not to be tolerated; but I know you will pardon it in me. Please answer it quickly as I feel impatient to know.

I have sent my love to your Fanny so often that I fear she is getting tired of it; however I venture to tender it again. Yours forever LINCOLN

PRINCIPLES

Lincoln thrived in the political world of the Illinois State legislature, but his ambition was such that he could not long remain satisfied as a local politician. He accordingly set his sights on the national stage, but when he sought the nomination as the Whig candidate for a seat in the United States Congress in 1843, he was defeated. In a letter to Martin Morris, a political supporter, Lincoln speculated on the impact of his political connections—and his religious beliefs—on the outcome of the election. Three years later Lincoln won his party's nomination for Congress. The ensuing campaign was unremarkable until his opponent accused Lincoln of being a "scoffer of Christianity." Lincoln's response to these "Charges of Infidelity" provide a rare glimpse into his views on religion and religious thought. Voters seemed little concerned with such accusations and Lincoln won the election easily, but his term in Congress was undistinguished and he returned to Springfield to face the very real possibility that his political career was at an end. By the early 1850s, it was clear that the Whig Party was disintegrating, further complicating Lincoln's political future. In an 1855 letter to his old friend, Joshua Speed, Lincoln reveals his uncertainties about his political affiliation even as his political values were beginning to come into sharper focus. But if his political future was uncertain, his legal career was thriving. By this time he had formed a clear opinion of what is required of the successful attorney, as shown in the notes he prepared for a lecture in the summer of 1850 and in a subsequent letter to Isham Reavis, who was seeking a legal career.

To Martin S. Morris, March 26, 1843

Springfield
March 26th. 1843

Friend Morris:

Your letter of the 23rd. was received on yesterday morning, and for which (instead of an excuse which you thought proper to ask) tender you my sincere thanks. It is truly gratifying to me to learn that while the people of Sangamon have cast me off, my old friends of Menard who have known me longest and best of any, still retain there confidence in me. It would astonish if not amuse, the older citizens of your County who twelve years ago knew me a strange[r], friendless, uneducated, penniless boy, working on a flat boat---at ten dollars per month to learn that I have been put down here as the candidate of pride, wealth, and arristocratic family distinction. Yet so chiefly it was. There was too the strangest combination of church influence against me. Baker is a Campbellite, and therefore as I supose, with few acceptions got all that church. My wife has some relatives in the Presbyterian and some in the Episcopal Churches, and therefore, whereever it would tell, I was set down as either the one or the other, whilst it was every where contended that no ch[r]istian ought to go for me, because I belonged to no church, was suspected of being a deist, and had talked about fighting a duel. With all these things Baker, of course had nothing to do. Nor do I complain of them. As to his own church going for him, I think that was right enough, and as to the influences I have spoken of in the other, though they were very strong, it would be grossly untrue and unjust to charge that they acted upon them in a body or even very nearly so. I only mean that those influences levied a tax of a considerable per cent. upon my strength throughout the religious comunity.

But enough of this. You say that in choosing a candidate for Congress you have an equal right with Sangamon, and in this you are undoubtedly correct. In agreeing to withdraw if the whigs of Sangamon should go against me I did not mean that they alone were worth consulting; but that if she with her heavy delegation should be against me, it would be impossible for me to succeed---and therefore I had as well decline. And in relation to Menard having rights, permit me to fully recognize them---and to express the opinion that if she and Mason act circumspectly they will in the convention be able so far to enforce there rights as to decide absolutely which one of the candidates shall be successful. Let me show you the reason of this. Hardin or some other Morgan Candidate will get Morgan, Scott, & Cass---14 Baker has Sangamon already, and he or he and some [one] else not the Morgan man will get Putnam, Marshall, Woodford, Taz[e]well & Logan---which with Sangamon make 16. Then you & Mason having three, can give the victory to either man. You say you shall instruct your delegates to go for me unless I object. I certainly shall not object. That would be too plesant a compliment for me to tread in the dust. And besides if any thing should hapen (which however is not probable) by which Baker should be thrown out of the fight, I would be at liberty to accept the nomination if I could get it. I do however feell myself bound not to hinder him in any way from getting the nomination. I should dispise myself were I to attempt it. I think it would be proper for your meeting to appoint three delegates, and instruct them to go for some one as first choice, some one else as second choice, and perhaps some one as third---and if in those instructions I were named as the first choice, it would gratify me very much. If you wish to hold the ballance of power, it is important for you to attend too, and secure the vote of Mason also. You should be sure to have men appointed delegates, that you know you can safely confide in. If yourself & James Short were appointed for your County all would be safe. But whether Jims woman afair a year ago might not be in the way of his appointment is a question. I dont know whether you know it, but I know him to be as honorable a man as there is in the world. You have my permission and even request to show this letter to Short; but to no one else unless it be a very particular friend who you know will not speak of it. Yours as ever

A. LINCOLN
P.S. Will you write me again? A. L---

Handbill Replying to Charges of Infidelity, July 31, 1846

To the Voters of the Seventh Congressional District.

FELLOW CITIZENS:

A charge having got into circulation in some of the neighborhoods of this District, in substance that I am an open scoffer at Christianity, I have by the advice of some friends concluded to notice the subject in this form. That I am not a member of any Christian Church, is true; but I have never denied the truth of the Scriptures; and I have never spoken with intentional disrespect of religion in general, or of any denomination of Christians in particular. It is true that in early life I was inclined to believe in what I understand is called the "Doctrine of Necessity"---that is, that the human mind is impelled to action, or held in rest by some power, over which the mind itself has no control; and I have sometimes (with one, two or three, but never publicly) tried to maintain this opinion in argument. The habit of arguing thus however, I have, entirely left off for more than five years. And I add here, I have always understood this same opinion to be held by several of the Christian denominations. The foregoing, is the whole truth, briefly stated, in relation to myself, upon this subject.

I do not think I could myself, be brought to support a man for office, whom I knew to be an open enemy of, and scoffer at, religion. Leaving the higher matter of eternal consequences, between him and his Maker, I still do not think any man has the right thus to insult the feelings, and injure the morals, of the community in which he may live. If, then, I was guilty of such conduct, I should blame no man who should condemn me for it; but I do blame those, whoever they may be, who falsely put such a charge in circulation against me.

July 31, 1846. A. LINCOLN.

Fragment: Notes for a Law Lecture, July 1, 1850 [?]

[July 1, 1850?]

I am not an accomplished lawyer. I find quite as much material for a lecture in those points wherein I have failed, as in those wherein I have been moderately successful. The leading rule for the lawyer, as for the man of every other calling, is diligence. Leave nothing for to-morrow which can be done to-day. Never let your correspondence fall behind. Whatever piece of business you have in hand, before stopping, do all the labor pertaining to it which can then be done. When you bring a common-law suit, if you have the facts for doing so, write the declaration at once. If a law point be involved, examine the books, and note the authority you rely on upon the declaration itself, where you are sure to find it when wanted. The same of defenses and pleas. In business not likely to be litigated,---ordinary collection cases, foreclosures, partitions, and the like,---make all examinations of titles, and note them, and even draft orders and decrees in advance. This course has a triple advantage; it avoids omissions and neglect, saves your labor when once done, performs the labor out of court when you have leisure, rather than in court when you have not. Extemporaneous speaking should be practised and cultivated. It is the lawyer's avenue to the public. However able and faithful he may be in other respects, people are slow to bring him business if he cannot make a speech. And yet there is not a more fatal error to young lawyers than relying too much on speech-making. If any one, upon his rare powers of speaking, shall claim an exemption from the drudgery of the law, his case is a failure in advance.

Discourage litigation. Persuade your neighbors to compromise whenever you can. Point out to them how the nominal winner is often a real loser---in fees, expenses, and waste of time. As a peacemaker the lawyer has a superior opportunity of being a good man. There will still be business enough.

Never stir up litigation. A worse man can scarcely be found than one who does this. Who can be more nearly a fiend than he who habitually overhauls the register of deeds in search of defects in titles, whereon to stir up strife, and put money in his pocket? A moral tone ought to be infused into the profession which should drive such men out of it.

The matter of fees is important, far beyond the mere question of bread and butter involved. Properly attended to, fuller justice is done to both lawyer and client. An exorbitant fee should never be claimed. As a general rule never take your whole fee in advance, nor any more than a small retainer. When fully paid beforehand, you are more than a common mortal if you can feel the same interest in the case, as if something was still in prospect for you, as well as for your client. And when you lack interest in the case the job will very likely lack skill and diligence in the performance. Settle the amount of fee and take a note in advance. Then you will feel that you are working for something, and you are sure to do your work faithfully and well. Never sell a fee note---at least not before the consideration service is performed. It leads to negligence and dishonesty---negligence by losing interest in the case, and dishonesty in refusing to refund when you have allowed the consideration to fail.

There is a vague popular belief that lawyers are necessarily dishonest. I say vague, because when we consider to what extent confidence and honors are reposed in and conferred upon lawyers by the people, it appears improbable that their impression of dishonesty is very distinct and vivid. Yet the impression is common, almost universal. Let no young man choosing the law for a calling for a moment yield to the popular belief---resolve to be honest at all events; and if in your own judgment you cannot be an honest lawyer, resolve to be honest without being a lawyer. Choose some other occupation, rather than one in the choosing of which you do, in advance, consent to be a knave.

To Joshua F. Speed, August 24, 1855

Springfield, Aug: 24, 1855

Dear Speed:

You know what a poor correspondent I am. Ever since I received your very agreeable letter of the 22nd. of May I have been intending to write you in answer to it. You suggest that in political action now, you and I would differ. I suppose we would; not quite as much, however, as you may think. You know I dislike slavery; and you fully admit the abstract wrong of it. So far there is no cause of difference. But you say that sooner than yield your legal right to the slave---especially at the bidding of those who are not themselves interested, you would see the Union dissolved. I am not aware that any one is bidding you to yield that right; very certainly I am not. I leave that matter entirely to yourself. I also acknowledge your rights and my obligations, under the constitution, in regard to your slaves. I confess I hate to see the poor creatures hunted down, and caught, and carried back to their stripes, and unrewarded toils; but I bite my lip and keep quiet. In 1841 you and I had together a tedious low-water trip, on a Steam Boat from Louisville to St. Louis. You may remember, as I well do, that from Louisville to the mouth of the Ohio there were, on board, ten or a dozen slaves, shackled together with irons. That sight was a continual torment to me; and I see something like it every time I touch the Ohio, or any other slave-border. It is hardly fair for you to assume, that I have no interest in a thing which has, and continually exercises, the power of making me miserable. You ought rather to appreciate how much the great body of the Northern people do crucify their feelings, in order to maintain their loyalty to the constitution and the Union.

I do oppose the extension of slavery, because my judgment and feelings so prompt me; and I am under no obligation to the contrary. If for this you and I must differ, differ we must. You say if you were President, you would send an army and hang the leaders of the Missouri outrages upon the Kansas elections; still, if Kansas fairly votes herself a slave state, she must be admitted, or the Union must be dissolved. But how if she votes herself a slave state unfairly---that is, by the very means for which you say you would hang men? Must she still be admitted, or the Union be dissolved? That will be the phase of the question when it first becomes a practical one. In your assumption that there may be a fair decision of the slavery question in Kansas, I plainly see you and I would differ about the Nebraska-law. I look upon that enactment not as a law, but as violence from the beginning. It was conceived in violence, passed in violence, is maintained in violence, and is being executed in violence. I say it was conceived in violence, because the destruction of the Missouri Compromise, under the circumstances, was nothing less than violence. It was passed in violence, because it could not have passed at all but for the votes of many members, in violent disregard of the known will of their constituents. It is maintained in violence because the elections since, clearly demand it's repeal, and this demand is openly disregarded. You say men ought to be hung for the way they are executing that law; and I say the way it is being executed is quite as good as any of its antecedents. It is being executed in the precise way which was intended from the first; else why does no Nebraska man express astonishment or condemnation? Poor Reeder is the only public man who has been silly enough to believe that any thing like fairness was ever intended; and he has been bravely undeceived.

That Kansas will form a Slave constitution, and, with it, will ask to be admitted into the Union, I take to be an already settled question; and so settled by the very means you so pointedly condemn. By every principle of law, ever held by any court, North or South, every negro taken to Kansas is free; yet in utter disregard of this---in the spirit of violence merely---that beautiful Legislature gravely passes a law to hang men who shall venture to inform a negro of his legal rights. This is the substance, and real object of the law. If, like Haman, they should hang upon the gallows of their own building, I shall not be among the mourners for their fate.

In my humble sphere, I shall advocate the restoration of the Missouri Compromise, so long as Kansas remains a territory; and when, by all these foul means, it seeks to come into the Union as a Slave-state, I shall oppose it. I am very loth, in any case, to withhold my assent to the enjoyment of property acquired, or located, in good faith; but I do not admit that good faith, in taking a negro to Kansas, to be held in slavery, is a possibility with any man. Any man who has sense enough to be the controller of his own property, has too much sense to misunderstand the outrageous character of this whole Nebraska business. But I digress. In my opposition to the admission of Kansas I shall have some company; but we may be beaten. If we are, I shall not, on that account, attempt to dissolve the Union. On the contrary, if we succeed, there will be enough of us to take care of the Union. I think it probable, however, we shall be beaten. Standing as a unit among yourselves, you can, directly, and indirectly, bribe enough of our men to carry the day---as you could on an open proposition to establish monarchy. Get hold of some man in the North, whose position and ability is such, that he can make the support of your measure---whatever it may be---a democratic party necessity, and the thing is done. Appropos of this, let me tell you an anecdote. Douglas introduced the Nebraska bill in January. In February afterwards, there was a call session of the Illinois Legislature. Of the one hundred members composing the two branches of that body, about seventy were democrats. These latter held a caucus, in which the Nebraska bill was talked of, if not formally discussed. It was thereby discovered that just three, and no more, were in favor of the measure. In a day or two Douglas' orders came on to have resolutions passed approving the bill; and they were passed by large majorities!!! The truth of this is vouched for by a bolting democratic member. The masses too, democratic as well as whig, were even, nearer unanamous against it; but as soon as the party necessity of supporting it, became apparent, the way the democracy began to see the wisdom and justice of it, was perfectly astonishing.

You say if Kansas fairly votes herself a free state, as a christian you will rather rejoice at it. All decent slave-holders talk that way; and I do not doubt their candor. But they never vote that way. Although in a private letter, or conversation, you will express your preference that Kansas shall be free, you would vote for no man for Congress who would say the same thing publicly. No such man could be elected from any district in any slave-state. You think Stringfellow & Co ought to be hung; and yet, at the next presidential election you will vote for the exact type and representative of Stringfellow. The slave-breeders and slave-traders, are a small, odious and detested class, among you; and yet in politics, they dictate the course of all of you, and are as completely your masters, as you are the masters of your own negroes.

You enquire where I now stand. That is a disputed point. I think I am a whig; but others say there are no whigs, and that I am an abolitionist. When I was at Washington I voted for the Wilmot Proviso as good as forty times, and I never heard of any one attempting to unwhig me for that. I now do no more than oppose the extension of slavery.

I am not a Know-Nothing. That is certain. How could I be? How can any one who abhors the oppression of negroes, be in favor of degrading classes of white people? Our progress in degeneracy appears to me to be pretty rapid. As a nation, we began by declaring that "all men are created equal." We now practically read it "all men are created equal, except negroes." When the Know-Nothings get control, it will read "all men are created equal, except negroes, and foreigners, and catholics." When it comes to this I should prefer emigrating to some country where they make no pretence of loving liberty---to Russia, for instance, where despotism can be taken pure, and without the base alloy of hypocracy.

Mary will probably pass a day or two in Louisville in October. My kindest regards to Mrs. Speed. On the leading subject of this letter, I have more of her sympathy than I have of yours.

And yet let [me] say I am Your friend forever

A. LINCOLN---

To Isham Reavis, November 5, 1855

Springfield, Novr. 5- 1855

Isham Reavis, Esq.

My dear Sir:

I have just reached home, and found your letter of the 23rd. ult. I am from home too much of my time, for a young man to read law with me advantageously. If you are resolutely determined to make a lawyer of yourself, the thing is more than half done already. It is but a small matter whether you read with any body or not. I did not read with any one. Get the books, and read and study them till, you understand them in their principal features; and that is the main thing. It is of no consequence to be in a large town while you are reading. I read at New-Salem, which never had three hundred people living in it. The books, and your capacity for understanding them, are just the same in all places. Mr. Dummer is a very clever man and an excellent lawyer (much better than I, in law-learning); and I have no doubt he will cheerfully tell you what books to read, and also loan you the books.

Always bear in mind that your own resolution to succeed, is more important than any other one thing.

Very truly Your friend

A. LINCOLN

From *Collected Works*. Abraham Lincoln Association, Springfield, IL. Roy P. Basler, editor; Marion Dolores Pratt and Lloyd A. Dunlap, assistant editors. Lincoln, Abraham, 1809-1865. New Brunswick, N.J.: Rutgers University Press, 1953. Copyright © The Abraham Lincoln Association. Reprinted by permission.

Part Two

Lincoln and Slavery

Lincoln claimed in 1858 that he had "always hated slavery." He might have added, however, that his views about ending slavery, or even about slaves themselves, had not always been so consistent. In fact, Lincoln's views on the institution of slavery evolved over the years. His first public opposition to slavery came in 1837 as a young state legislator in Illinois, but by 1865 that opposition had grown into a focused and determined campaign to amend the Constitution and end slavery altogether.

The earliest influence on Lincoln's views regarding slavery was probably his father, Thomas Lincoln, who was said to have moved his family from Kentucky to Indiana, in part, because of his distaste for slavery. Once established in Indiana, however, it is not clear that any of the Lincolns thought much about slavery until 1828, when Abraham Lincoln took a job as a deckhand on a flatboat headed down the Mississippi River to New Orleans. His voyage in that year, together with a second trip three years later, coincided with the first frantic growth of slavery in the new states of the Deep South, and that experience must have intensified his opposition to slavery.

The growth of the Abolitionist movement and the resulting national debate on slavery compelled Lincoln, along with the rest of the country, to re-examine his position on the institution. By that time, Lincoln was a successful politician and a rising young attorney, and those factors no doubt influenced and perhaps tempered the intensity of his opposition to slavery. As a politician, he was aware that many of his constituents who condemned the institution of slavery held little sympathy for the slaves as individuals. Indeed, it may be that Lincoln himself shared this position. Certainly his early statements about slaves gave little indication that he believed them to be capable—or perhaps even worthy—of social or political equality in the United States. Equally certain is that neither Lincoln nor most of his constituents were inclined to endorse what they saw as a radical solution proposed by the Abolitionists to end slavery immediately and unconditionally.

As a lawyer, Lincoln's position on slavery was less ambiguous. He was sworn to uphold the laws of the court and there was no higher law in the land than the U.S. Constitution, a document that recognized and protected slavery. Lincoln was thus obliged to accept the fact that slavery was legal. Even so, he felt compelled to understand why the framers of the Constitution would have allowed such an evil institution to continue. He explained this to himself and to others by arguing that even in 1787, when the Constitution was written, it was apparent that slavery was not suitable to certain areas of the country. If it could be contained in the South where it already existed, slavery must eventually become unprofitable and unsupportable, and must therefore come to an end.

Yet Lincoln also believed that slavery's end could be hastened, and toward that objective he was a strong supporter of the colonization movement. His support for the scheme of relocating freed slaves to Africa was no doubt influenced by his political idol Henry Clay, who was himself a slaveholder but was at the same time a strong supporter of colonization. In fact, during the early- to mid-nineteenth century, colonization was seen by many in the north as the best solution to the slavery question. It was a solution, however, that was itself plagued with problems, not the least of which was that Southern slave-owners must first agree to free their slaves, which they were unlikely to do without some form of compensation.

Lincoln's support for colonization continued well into his presidency, but it was never as intense or strident as his opposition to the extension of slavery into the western territories. He grudgingly accepted that he must tolerate slavery where it existed and was constitutionally protected, but he was adamant that it not extend into places where it had never existed. Such an eventuality was not possible so long as the Missouri Compromise was in place and continued, as it had since 1820, to define the boundaries between free states and slave states for a growing nation. The situation changed dramatically in 1854, however, with the passage of the Kansas-Nebraska Act. Contained within that act was the provision that the Missouri Compromise be repealed, creating the possibility that slavery could extend anywhere in the new territories or, for that matter, anywhere in the nation. Lincoln, whose political career had been uncertain, now became one of the foremost critics of the Kansas-Nebraska Act. He spoke out against it at every opportunity and directed much of his anger at Stephen Douglas, a United States Senator from Illinois and the sponsor of the act. By October of that year, when he stood before a crowd at Peoria, Illinois, Lincoln's opposition to the act was refined and well-organized. The speech he delivered that day reflects a dramatic shift in his writing. Already precise and effective, Lincoln's words now carried a new sense of moral urgency and the result is captivating and persuasive.

Lincoln was not alone in his outrage over the Kansas-Nebraska Act. By 1855, a variety of political groups and organizations with little in common other than their opposition to the act, coalesced into a new political party, the Republicans. Lincoln too joined the Republicans and when Douglas ran for re-election in 1858, Lincoln secured the Republican nomination to run against him. The central part of the ensuing campaign was a series of seven debates between the two candidates, and the central theme of the debates was the Kansas-Nebraska Act. Not surprisingly, the debates often turned to other aspects of slavery such as the prospect of Black equality, and here Lincoln seemed less comfortable. On the central issue, however, Lincoln was clear; slavery, he admitted, could not be attacked in the South where it was established but it must not be allowed to extend into the territories. On this point Lincoln was forceful and unwavering.

Lincoln held his own against Douglas, one of the nation's most celebrated orators, and actually won the popular vote in the election. Even so, Democrats retained control of the Illinois legislature and thereby ensured that Douglas retained his seat in the Senate. Yet even though Lincoln lost the election, he gained national recognition as a fresh and dynamic opponent of the Kansas-Nebraska Act. In early 1860, on the basis of this new notoriety, he was invited to speak in New York City at Cooper Union Hall. Lincoln recognized that his audience would include influential party leaders as well as reporters from every major newspaper in the Northeast, and he took great pains to research and prepare his remarks. The result was a speech that reflected his views on slavery at that point in his life: first, he showed that the founders had never intended for the nation to endure half-slave and half-free; then, he reminded the South that the Republican Party was no threat to slavery there, but—in his final point—he once again stated that slavery must not be allowed to expand into the territories.

Lincoln's Cooper Union Address propelled him into serious contention for the Republican nomination, which he won three months later at the Republican Convention in Chicago. Running against a divided Democratic Party, Lincoln and his fellow Republicans recognized that his chances for victory were very good. They were correct, and Lincoln was elected to the Presidency in November 1860. In his first year as president, Lincoln held to the Republican Party platform with regard to slavery; indeed, as president he was constitutionally prohibited from interfering with slavery where it already existed. But by the summer of 1862 he came to recognize that, as commander-in-chief, he could attack slavery as a military objective and not run afoul of the Constitution. In fact, Lincoln came to believe that not only was such an approach permissible, it was essential to saving the Union. According to Gideon Welles, Lincoln's Secretary of the Navy, Lincoln had come to the conclusion in July that it was necessary to "free the slaves or be ourselves subdued."[1]

Lincoln was, by that time, probably already working on a preliminary version of the Emancipation Proclamation, and presented a draft of that document to his cabinet in August. There was little dissent among the cabinet members but, led by Secretary of State William Seward, they did persuade Lincoln not to release the document to the public until Union armies achieved a significant victory on the battlefield. That victory came in September at Antietam and five days later a preliminary version of the Emancipation Proclamation was announced. Clearly a war measure, the Proclamation was set to go into effect on January 1, 1863, and only freed slaves in areas that were still in rebellion at that time. Still, it represented a major departure from previous federal policy toward slavery and a major turning point in Lincoln's own attitude toward slavery.

The next challenge for Lincoln was to give the proclamation some permanency. As a presidential proclamation, it was subject to being overturned by a future president or simply expiring when it was no longer deemed necessary as part of the war effort. Lincoln needed a Constitutional Amendment that permanently abolished slavery. By the end of that year, Congress began to debate such an amendment and the Senate version passed in April 1864. The House, however, refused to pass the Senate bill and thus the issue came to a close for the moment. Not until the following year did the House return to the issue, and even then only because of pressure from Lincoln himself. But Lincoln's efforts were successful, and in February the House passed the Thirteenth Amendment. It was still necessary to secure ratification from the states, but Lincoln knew that the end of slavery was at hand. The institution that he had hated throughout his life but had seemed impossible to destroy had at last been dealt a mortal blow.

---

1 Gideon Welles, *Diary of Gideon Welles, Secretary of the Navy Under Lincoln and Johnson* (New York: Houghton-Mifflin, 1911), I:70-71.

Lincoln understood that the end of slavery brought freedom but it did not necessarily create equality or acceptance. He urged Congress to pass legislation ensuring federal support in the transition from slavery to freedom. The result was the Freedmen's Bureau Bill that passed in March 1865. Yet the most profound transition envisioned by Lincoln was the move to citizenship, something he had come to recognize as an essential step in what was bound to be a difficult journey for Blacks as they assumed a new place in American society. On several occasions in the last few months of his life, Lincoln called for some form of Black suffrage but how he intended to realize this objective is impossible to know.

Lincoln's attitude toward slaves and slavery itself evolved throughout his life, culminating in his role as the "Great Emancipator" and the architect of what he called a "new birth of freedom." His vision of a future in which equal opportunity, including the right to vote, was a reality for all Americans regardless of color lost its greatest and most able champion when Lincoln was assassinated. The persuasive voice that had successfully inspired the nation to persevere and endure the hardships and sacrifices of war in order to save the Union was absent during Reconstruction. African-Americans eventually entered into a period known as the "long night" of discrimination, exploitation, and humiliation that lasted for almost a century before even a semblance of Lincoln's vision was realized.

EARLY VIEWS

Lincoln's first publicly expressed opposition to slavery was in 1837. In March of that year, he and a fellow legislator formally protested a recent resolution by the Illinois General Assembly condemning Abolition societies. The tone of his protest seems to confirm Lincoln's hatred of the institution, yet four years later, in a letter to the sister of his close friend Joshua Speed, Lincoln casually describes a close encounter with chained slaves and emphasizes their apparent happiness. By the time he arrived in Washington D.C. to take his seat in Congress, Lincoln was convinced that Congress had the authority to abolish slavery within the District of Columbia and he attempted to rally support for an earlier resolution calling for such action. His proposed amendments failed to generate much enthusiasm and his promise to introduce a different version of the same bill met with even less interest. His single term in Congress came to an end later that year, and when he returned to Springfield it seemed as if his political career was at an end as well. Instead, as the national debate over extending slavery into the western territories intensified, Lincoln became politically re-energized. There are at least two "fragments on slavery" prepared sometime in the spring or early summer of 1854, which reflect his renewed focus on politics and his belief that slavery, and especially the growth of slavery, represented a dire threat to the very fabric of the nation. In the first fragment, Lincoln explains his position that slavery is essentially based on greed and selfishness by the owners and that no slave could possibly fail to understand that he or she is being wronged and exploited. In the second fragment, Lincoln presents a very logical argument that no person could be exempted from the possibility of slavery if rules are defined by the most powerful persons.

Protest in the Illinois Legislature on Slavery, March 3, 1837

March 3, 1837

The following protest was presented to the House, which was read and ordered to be spread on the journals, to wit:

"Resolutions upon the subject of domestic slavery having passed both branches of the General Assembly at its present session, the undersigned hereby protest against the passage of the same.

They believe that the institution of slavery is founded on both injustice and bad policy; but that the promulgation of abolition doctrines tends rather to increase than to abate its evils.

They believe that the Congress of the United States has no power, under the constitution, to interfere with the institution of slavery in the different States.

They believe that the Congress of the United States has the power, under the constitution, to abolish slavery in the District of Columbia; but that that power ought not to be exercised unless at the request of the people of said District.

The difference between these opinions and those contained in the said resolutions, is their reason for entering this protest."

DAN STONE,

A. LINCOLN,

Representatives from the county of Sangamon.

To Mary Speed, September 27, 1841

Miss Mary Speed, Bloomington, Illinois,

Louisville, Ky. Sept. 27th. 1841

My Friend: Having resolved to write to some of your mother's family, and not having the express permission of any one of them [to] do so, I have had some little difficulty in determining on which to inflict the task of reading what I now feel must be a most dull and silly letter; but when I remembered that you and I were something of cronies while I was at Farmington, and that, while there, I once was under the necessity of shutting you up in a room to prevent your committing an assault and battery upon me, I instantly decided that you should be the devoted one.

I assume that you have not heard from Joshua & myself since we left, because I think it doubtful whether he has written.

You remember there was some uneasiness about Joshua's health when we left. That little indisposition of his turned out to be nothing serious; and it was pretty nearly forgotten when we reached Springfield. We got on board the Steam Boat Lebanon, in the locks of the Canal about 12. o'clock. M. of the day we left, and reached St. Louis the next monday at 8 P.M. Nothing of interest happened during the passage, except the vexatious delays occasioned by the sand bars be thought interesting. By the way, a fine example was presented on board the boat for contemplating the effect of condition upon human happiness. A gentleman had purchased twelve negroes in different parts of Kentucky and was taking them to a farm in the South. They were chained six and six together. A small iron clevis was around the left wrist of each, and this fastened to the main chain by a shorter one at a convenient distance from, the others; so that the negroes were strung together precisely like so many fish upon a trot-line. In this condition they were being separated forever from the scenes of their childhood, their friends, their fathers and mothers, and brothers and sisters, and many of them, from their wives and children, and going into perpetual slavery where the lash of the master is proverbially more ruthless and unrelenting than any other where; and yet amid all these distressing circumstances, as we would think them, they were the most cheerful and apparantly happy creatures on board. One, whose offence for which he had been sold was an over-fondness for his wife, played the fiddle almost continually; and the others danced, sung, cracked jokes, and played various games with cards from day to day. How true it is that "God tempers the wind to the shorn lamb," or in other words, that He renders the worst of human conditions tolerable, while He permits the best, to be nothing better than tolerable.

To return to the narative. When we reached Springfield, I staid but one day when I started on this tedious circuit where I now am. Do you remember my going to the city while I was in Kentucky, to have a tooth extracted, and making a failure of it? Well, that same old tooth got to paining me so much, that about a week since I had it torn out, bringing with it a bit of the jawbone; the consequence of which is that my mouth is now so sore that I can neither talk, nor eat. I am litterally "subsisting on savoury remembrances"---that is, being unable to eat, I am living upon the remembrance of the delicious dishes of peaches and cream we used to have at your house.

When we left, Miss Fanny Henning was owing you a visit, as I understood. Has she paid it yet? If she has, are you not convinced that she is one of the sweetest girls in the world? There is but one thing about her, so far as I could perceive, that I would have otherwise than as it is. That is something of a tendency to mellancholly. This, let it be observed, is a misfortune not a fault. Give her an assurance of my verry highest regard, when you see her.

Is little Siss Eliza Davis at your house yet? If she is kiss her "o'er and o'er again" for me.

Tell your mother that I have not got her "present" with me; but that I intend to read it regularly when I return home. I doubt not that it is really, as she says, the best cure for the "Blues" could one but take it according to the truth.

Give my respects to all your sisters (including "Aunt Emma") and brothers. Tell Mrs. Peay, of whose happy face I shall long retain a pleasant remembrance, that I have been trying to think of a name for her homestead, but as yet, can not satisfy myself with one. I shall be verry happy to receive a line from you, soon after you receive this; and, in case you choose to favour me with one, address it to Charleston, Coles Co. Ills as I shall be there about the time to receive it. Your sincere friend

A. LINCOLN

Remarks and Resolution Introduced in United States House of Representatives Concerning Abolition of Slavery in the District of Columbia

January 10, 1849

Mr. LINCOLN appealed to his colleague [Mr. WENTWORTH] to withdraw his motion, to enable him to read a proposition which he intended to submit, if the vote should be reconsidered.

Mr. WENTWORTH again withdrew his motion for that purpose.

Mr. LINCOLN said, that by the courtesy of his colleague, he would say, that if the vote on the resolution was reconsidered, he should make an effort to introduce an amendment, which he should now read.

And Mr. L. read as follows:
Strike out all before and after the word "Resolved" and insert the following, towit: That the Committee on the District of Columbia be instructed to report a bill in substance as follows, towit:

Section 1 Be it enacted by the Senate and House of Representatives of the United States of America, in Congress assembled: That no person not now within the District of Columbia, nor now owned by any person or persons now resident within it, nor hereafter born within it, shall ever be held in slavery within said District.

Section 2. That no person now within said District, or now owned by any person, or persons now resident within the same, or hereafter born within it, shall ever be held in slavery without the limits of said District: <u>Provided</u>, that officers of the government of the United States, being citizens of the slave-holding states, coming into said District on public business, and remaining only so long as may be reasonably necessary for that object, may be attended into, and out of, said District, and while there, by the necessary servants of themselves and their families, without their right to hold such servants in service, being thereby impaired.

Section 3. That all children born of slave mothers within said District on, or after the first day of January in the year of our Lord one thousand, eight hundred and fifty shall be free; but shall be reasonably supported and educated, by the respective owners of their mothers or by their heirs or representatives, and shall owe reasonable service, as apprentices, to such owners, heirs and representatives until they respectively arrive at the age of --- years when they shall be entirely free; and the municipal authorities of Washington and Georgetown, within their respective jurisdictional limits, are hereby empowered and required to make all suitable and necessary provisions for enforcing obedience to this section, on the part of both masters and apprentices.

Section 4. That all persons now within said District lawfully held as slaves, or now owned by any person or persons now resident within said District, shall remain such, at the will of their respective owners, their heirs and legal representatives: <u>Provided</u> that any such owner, or his legal representative, may at any time receive from the treasury of the United States the full value of his or her slave, of the class in this section mentioned, upon which such slave shall be forthwith and forever free: and <u>provided further</u> that the President of the United States, the Secretary of State, and the Secretary of the Treasury shall be a board for determining the value of such slaves as their owners may desire to emancipate under this section; and whose duty it shall be to hold a session for the purpose, on the first monday of each calendar month; to receive all applications; and, on satisfactory evidence in each case, that the person presented for valuation, is a slave, and of the class in this section mentioned, and is owned by the applicant, shall value such slave at his or her full cash value, and give to the applicant an order on the treasury for the amount; and also to such slave a certificate of freedom.

Section 5 That the municipal authorities of Washington and Georgetown, within their respective jurisdictional limits, are hereby empowered and required to provide active and efficient means to arrest, and deliver up to their owners, all fugitive slaves escaping into said District.

Section 6 That the election officers within said District of Columbia, are hereby empowered and required to open polls at all the usual places of holding elections, on the first monday of April next, and receive the vote of every free white male citizen above the age of twentyone years, having resided within said District for the period of one year or more next preceding the time of such voting, for, or against this act; to proceed, in taking said votes, in all respects not herein specified, as at elections under the municipal laws; and, with as little delay as possible, to transmit correct statements of the votes so cast to the President of the United States. And it shall be the duty of the President to canvass said votes immediately, and, if a majority of them be found to be for this act, to forthwith issue his proclamation giving notice of the fact; and this act shall only be in full force and effect on, and after the day of such proclamation.

Section 7. That involuntary servitude for the punishment of crime, whereof the party shall have been duly convicted shall in no wise be prohibited by this act.

Section 8. That for all the purposes of this act the jurisdictional limits of Washington are extended to all parts of the District of Columbia not now included within the present limits of Georgetown.

Mr. LINCOLN then said, that he was authorized to say, that of about fifteen of the leading citizens of the District of Columbia to whom this proposition had been submitted, there was not one but who approved of the adoption of such a proposition. He did not wish to be misunderstood. He did not know whether or not they would vote for this bill on the first Monday of April; but he repeated, that out of fifteen persons to whom it had been submitted, he had authority to say that every one of them desired that some proposition like this should pass.

From *Collected Works*. Abraham Lincoln Association, Springfield, IL. Roy P. Basler, editor; Marion Dolores Pratt and Lloyd A. Dunlap, assistant editors. Lincoln, Abraham, 1809-1865. New Brunswick, N.J.: Rutgers University Press, 1953. Copyright © The Abraham Lincoln Association. Reprinted by permission.

Fragments on Slavery, April 1[?], 1854

If A. can prove, however conclusively, that he may, of right, enslave B.---why may not B. snatch the same argument, and prove equally, that he may enslave A?---

You say A. is white, and B. is black. It is color, then; the lighter, having the right to enslave the darker? Take care. By this rule, you are to be slave to the first man you meet, with a fairer skin than your own.

You do not mean color exactly?---You mean the whites are intellectually the superiors of the blacks, and, therefore have the right to enslave them? Take care again. By this rule, you are to be slave to the first man you meet, with an intellect superior to your own.

But, say you, it is a question of interest; and, if you can make it your interest, you have the right to enslave another. Very well. And if he can make it his interest, he has the right to enslave you.

From *Collected Works*. Abraham Lincoln Association, Springfield, IL. Roy P. Basler, editor; Marion Dolores Pratt and Lloyd A. Dunlap, assistant editors. Lincoln, Abraham, 1809-1865. New Brunswick, N.J.: Rutgers University Press, 1953. Copyright © The Abraham Lincoln Association. Reprinted by permission.

ATTACKING SLAVERY

On October 16, 1854 Lincoln delivered a speech in Peoria, Illinois addressing questions related to the passage of the Kansas-Nebraska Act. The speech was widely covered by the newspapers and signaled the return of Abraham Lincoln from his self-imposed political exile. The following year, Lincoln wrote a letter to Judge George Robinson of Lexington, Kentucky, a prominent attorney who had represented the estate of Robert S. Todd, Lincoln's father-in-law, in various legal matters. The last two paragraphs of Lincoln's letter are extraordinarily revealing, in part because he anticipates a speech that he will deliver three years later when he accepts the Republican nomination to run against Stephen Douglas for the United States Senate. It was that speech, generally referred to as the "House Divided" speech, which gave Lincoln his first taste of national notoriety. But it was his series of debates with Douglas in the ensuing campaign that gave Lincoln real national exposure. Newspaper reporters from across the nation covered the debates, primarily because Douglas was the sponsor of the Kansas-Nebraska Act and was expected to run for the presidency in 1860. In the process, however, they noted the little-known Illinois lawyer who matched up well against Douglas, the "Little Giant," and by some estimates actually bested him. Lincoln had some awkward moments, however, as evidenced in the excerpt from the fourth debate in Charleston contained here. But there was nothing awkward about Lincoln's speech at the Cooper Union Hall in New York City in February 1860. Once again, reporters from every major East coast newspaper were in the audience. Also in attendance were several influential Republican leaders who were not satisfied with the radical views of the party's leading presidential nominees. A more moderate vice-presidential nominee might soften the ticket and improve their chances in the general election. Lincoln delivered a speech that not only satisfied the party leaders that he was an acceptable moderate, but was so masterful that he thereafter became a legitimate candidate for president in his own right. On the strength of that momentum, Lincoln gained the Republican nomination and, in November 1860, was elected president.

Speech at Peoria, Illinois (excerpts), October 16, 1854

The repeal of the Missouri Compromise, and the propriety of its restoration, constitute the subject of what I am about to say. . . . I do not propose to question the patriotism, or to assail the motives of any man, or class of men; but rather to strictly confine myself to the naked merits of the question.

I also wish to be no less than National in all the positions I may take; and whenever I take ground which others have thought, or may think, narrow, sectional and dangerous to the Union, I hope to give a reason, which will appear sufficient, at least to some, why I think differently.

And, as this subject is no other, than part and parcel of the larger general question of domestic-slavery, I wish to MAKE and to KEEP the distinction between the EXISTING institution, and the EXTENSION of it, so broad, and so clear, that no honest man can misunderstand me, and no dishonest one, successfully misrepresent me.

In order to [get?] a clear understanding of what the Missouri Compromise is, a short history of the preceding kindred subjects will perhaps be proper. When we established our independence, we did not own, or claim, the country to which this compromise applies. Indeed, strictly speaking, the confederacy then owned no country at all; the States respectively owned the country within their limits; and some of them owned territory beyond their strict State limits. Virginia thus owned the North-Western territory---the country out of which the principal part of Ohio, all Indiana, all

Illinois, all Michigan and all Wisconsin, have since been formed. She also owned (perhaps within her then limits) what has since been formed into the State of Kentucky. North Carolina thus owned what is now the State of Tennessee; and South Carolina and Georgia, in separate parts, owned what are now Mississippi and Alabama. Connecticut, I think, owned the little remaining part of Ohio---being the same where they now send Giddings to Congress, and beat all creation at making cheese. These territories, together with the States themselves, constituted all the country over which the confederacy then claimed any sort of jurisdiction. We were then living under the Articles of Confederation, which were superceded by the Constitution several years afterwards. The question of ceding these territories to the general government was set on foot. Mr. Jefferson, the author of the Declaration of Independence, and otherwise a chief actor in the revolution; then a delegate in Congress; afterwards twice President; who was, is, and perhaps will continue to be, the most distinguished politician of our history; a Virginian by birth and continued residence, and withal, a slave-holder; conceived the idea of taking that occasion, to prevent slavery ever going into the north-western territory. He prevailed on the Virginia Legislature to adopt his views, and to cede the territory, making the prohibition of slavery therein, a condition of the deed. Congress accepted the cession, with the condition; and in the first Ordinance (which the acts of Congress were then called) for the government of the territory, provided that slavery should never be permitted therein. This is the famed ordinance of '87 so often spoken of. Thenceforward, for sixty-one years, and until in 1848, the last scrap of this territory came into the Union as the State of Wisconsin, all parties acted in quiet obedience to this ordinance. It is now what Jefferson foresaw and intended---the happy home of teeming millions of free, white, prosperous people, and no slave amongst them.

Thus, with the author of the declaration of Independence, the policy of prohibiting slavery in new territory originated. Thus, away back of the constitution, in the pure fresh, free breath of the revolution, the State of Virginia, and the National congress put that policy in practice. Thus through sixty odd of the best years of the republic did that policy steadily work to its great and beneficent end. And thus, in those five states, and five millions of free, enterprising people, we have before us the rich fruits of this policy

But now new light breaks upon us. Now congress declares this ought never to have been; and the like of it, must never be again. The sacred right of self government is grossly violated by it! We even find some men, who drew their first breath, and every other breath of their lives, under this very restriction, now live in dread of absolute suffocation, if they should be restricted in the "sacred right" of taking slaves to Nebraska. That perfect liberty they sigh for---the liberty of making slaves of other people---Jefferson never thought of; their own father never thought of; they never thought of themselves, a year ago. How fortunate for them, they did not sooner become sensible of their great misery! Oh, how difficult it is to treat with respect, such assaults upon all we have ever really held sacred. . . .

. . . I think, and shall try to show, that it is wrong; wrong in its direct effect, letting slavery into Kansas and Nebraska---and wrong in its prospective principle, allowing it to spread to every other part of the wide world, where men can be found inclined to take it.

This declared indifference, but as I must think, covert real zeal for the spread of slavery, I can not but hate. I hate it because of the monstrous injustice of slavery itself. I hate it because it deprives our republican example of its just influence in the world---enables the enemies of free institutions, with plausibility, to taunt us as hypocrites---causes the real friends of freedom to doubt our sincerity, and especially because it forces so many really good men amongst ourselves into an open war with the very fundamental principles of civil liberty---criticising the Declaration of Independence, and insisting that there is no right principle of action but self-interest.

Before proceeding, let me say I think I have no prejudice against the Southern people. They are just what we would be in their situation. If slavery did not now exist amongst them, they would not introduce it. If it did now exist amongst us, we should not instantly give it up. This I believe of the masses north and south. Doubtless there are individuals, on both sides, who would not hold slaves under any circumstances; and others who would gladly introduce slavery anew, if it were out of existence. We know that some southern men do free their slaves, go north, and become tip-top abolitionists; while some northern ones go south, and become most cruel slave-masters.

When southern people tell us they are no more responsible for the origin of slavery, than we; I acknowledge the fact. When it is said that the institution exists; and that it is very difficult to get rid of it, in any satisfactory way, I can understand and appreciate the saying. I surely will not blame them for not doing what I should not know how to do myself. If all earthly power were given me, I should not know what to do, as to the existing institution. My first impulse would be to free all the slaves, and send them to Liberia,---to their own native land. But a moment's reflection would convince me, that whatever of high hope, (as I think there is) there may be in this, in the long run, its sudden execution is impossible. If they were all landed there in a day, they would all perish in the next ten days; and there are not surplus shipping and surplus money enough in the world to carry them there in many times ten days. What then? Free them all, and keep them among us as underlings? Is it quite certain that this betters their condition? I think I would not hold one in slavery, at any rate; yet the point is not clear enough for me to denounce people upon. What next? Free them, and make them politically and socially, our equals? My own feelings will not admit of this; and if mine would, we well know that those of the great mass of white people will not. Whether this feeling accords with justice and sound judgment, is not the sole question, if indeed, it is any part of it. A universal feeling, whether well or ill-founded, can not be safely disregarded. We can not, then, make them equals. It does seem to me that systems of gradual emancipation might be adopted; but for their tardiness in this, I will not undertake to judge our brethren of the south.

When they remind us of their constitutional rights, I acknowledge them, not grudgingly, but fully, and fairly; and I would give them any legislation for the reclaiming of their fugitives, which should not, in its stringency, be more likely to carry a free man into slavery, than our ordinary criminal laws are to hang an innocent one.

But all this; to my judgment, furnishes no more excuse for permitting slavery to go into our own free territory, than it would for reviving the African slave trade by law. The law which forbids the bringing of slaves from Africa; and that which has so long forbid the taking them to Nebraska, can hardly be distinguished on any moral principle; and the repeal of the former could find quite as plausible excuses as that of the latter. . . .

. . . But Nebraska is urged as a great Union-saving measure. Well I too, go for saving the Union. Much as I hate slavery, I would consent to the extension of it rather than see the Union dissolved, just as I would consent to any GREAT evil, to avoid a GREATER one. But when I go to Union saving, I must believe, at least, that the means I employ has some adaptation to the end. To my mind, Nebraska has no such adaptation.

"It hath no relish of salvation in it."

It is an aggravation, rather, of the only one thing which ever endangers the Union. When it came upon us, all was peace and quiet. The nation was looking to the forming of new bonds of Union; and a long course of peace and prosperity seemed to lie before us. In the whole range of possibility, there scarcely appears to me to have been any thing, out of which the slavery agitation could have been revived, except the very project of repealing the Missouri compromise. Every inch of territory we owned, already had a definite settlement of the slavery question, and by which, all parties were pledged to abide. Indeed, there was no uninhabited country on the continent, which we could acquire; if we except some extreme northern regions, which are wholly out of the question. In this state of case, the genius of Discord himself, could scarcely have invented a way of again getting [setting?] us by the ears, but by turning back and destroying the peace measures of the past. The councils of that genius seem to have prevailed, the Missouri compromise was repealed; and here we are, in the midst of a new slavery agitation, such, I think, as we have never seen before.

Who is responsible for this? Is it those who resist the measure; or those who, causelessly, brought it forward, and pressed it through, having reason to know, and, in fact, knowing it must and would be so resisted? It could not but be expected by its author, that it would be looked upon as a measure for the extension of slavery, aggravated by a gross breach of faith. Argue as you will, and long as you will, this is the naked FRONT and ASPECT, of the measure. And in this aspect, it could not but produce agitation. Slavery is founded in the selfishness of man's nature---opposition to it, is [in?] his love of justice. These principles are an eternal antagonism; and when brought into collision so fiercely, as slavery extension brings them, shocks, and throes, and convulsions must ceaselessly follow. Repeal the Missouri compromise---repeal all compromises---repeal the declaration of independence---repeal all past history, you still can not repeal human nature. It still will be the abundance of man's heart, that slavery extension is wrong; and out of the abundance of his heart, his mouth will continue to speak. . . .

. . . The Missouri Compromise ought to be restored. For the sake of the Union, it ought to be restored. We ought to elect a House of Representatives which will vote its restoration. If by any means, we omit to do this, what follows? Slavery may or may not be established in Nebraska. But whether it be or not, we shall have repudiated---discarded from the councils of the Nation---the SPIRIT of COMPROMISE; for who after this will ever trust in a national compromise? The spirit of mutual concession---that spirit which first gave us the constitution, and which has thrice saved the Union---we shall have strangled and cast from us forever. And what shall we have in lieu of it? The South flushed with triumph and tempted to excesses; the North, betrayed, as they believe, brooding on wrong and burning for revenge. One side will provoke; the other resent. The one will taunt, the other defy; one agrees [aggresses?], the other retaliates. Already a few in the North, defy all constitutional restraints, resist the execution of the fugitive slave law, and even menace the institution of slavery in the states where it exists.

Already a few in the South, claim the constitutional right to take to and hold slaves in the free states---demand the revival of the slave trade; and demand a treaty with Great Britain by which fugitive slaves may be reclaimed from Canada. As yet they are but few on either side. It is a grave question for the lovers of the Union, whether the final destruction of the Missouri Compromise, and with it the spirit of all compromise will or will not embolden and embitter each of these, and fatally increase the numbers of both.

But restore the compromise, and what then? We thereby restore the national faith, the national confidence, the national feeling of brotherhood. We thereby reinstate the spirit of concession and compromise---that spirit which has never failed us in past perils, and which may be safely trusted for all the future. The south ought to join in doing this. The peace of the nation is as dear to them as to us. In memories of the past and hopes of the future, they share as largely as we. It would be on their part, a great act---great in its spirit, and great in its effect. It would be worth to the nation a hundred years' purchase of peace and prosperity. And what of sacrifice would they make? They only surrender to us, what they gave us for a consideration long, long ago; what they have not now, asked for, struggled or cared for; what has been thrust upon them, not less to their own astonishment than to ours.

But it is said we cannot restore it; that though we elect every member of the lower house, the Senate is still against us. It is quite true, that of the Senators who passed the Nebraska bill, a majority of the whole Senate will retain their seats in spite of the elections of this and the next year. But if at these elections, their several constituencies shall clearly express their will against Nebraska, will these senators disregard their will? Will they neither obey, nor make room for those who will?

But even if we fail to technically restore the compromise, it is still a great point to carry a popular vote in favor of the restoration. The moral weight of such a vote can not be estimated too highly. The authors of Nebraska are not at all satisfied with the destruction of the compromise---an endorsement of this PRINCIPLE, they proclaim to be the great object. With them, Nebraska alone is a small matter---to establish a principle, for FUTURE USE, is what they particularly desire.

That future use is to be the planting of slavery wherever in the wide world, local and unorganized opposition can not prevent it. Now if you wish to give them this endorsement---if you wish to establish this principle---do so. I shall regret it; but it is your right. On the contrary if you are opposed to the principle---intend to give it no such endorsement---let no wheedling, no sophistry, divert you from throwing a direct vote against it.

Some men, mostly whigs, who condemn the repeal of the Missouri Compromise, nevertheless hesitate to go for its restoration, lest they be thrown in company with the abolitionist. Will they allow me as an old whig to tell them good humoredly, that I think this is very silly? Stand with anybody that stands RIGHT. Stand with him while he is right and PART with him when he goes wrong. Stand WITH the abolitionist in restoring the Missouri Compromise; and stand AGAINST him when he attempts to repeal the fugitive slave law. In the latter case you stand with the southern disunionist. What of that? you are still right. In both cases you are right. In both cases you oppose [expose?] the dangerous extremes. In both you stand on middle ground and hold the ship level and steady. In both you are national and nothing less than national. This is good old whig ground. To desert such ground, because of any company, is to be less than a whig---less than a man---less than an American.

I particularly object to the NEW position which the avowed principle of this Nebraska law gives to slavery in the body politic. I object to it because it assumes that there CAN be MORAL RIGHT in the enslaving of one man by another. I object to it as a dangerous dalliance for a few [free?] people---a sad evidence that, feeling prosperity we forget right---that liberty, as a principle, we have ceased to revere. I object to it because the fathers of the republic eschewed, and rejected it. The argument of "Necessity" was the only argument they ever admitted in favor of slavery; and so far, and so far only as it carried them, did they ever go. They found the institution existing among us, which they could not help; and they cast blame upon the British King for having permitted its introduction. BEFORE the constitution, they prohibited its introduction into the north-western

Territory---the only country we owned, then free from it. AT the framing and adoption of the constitution, they forbore to so much as mention the word "slave" or "slavery" in the whole instrument. In the provision for the recovery of fugitives, the slave is spoken of as a "PERSON HELD TO SERVICE OR LABOR." In that prohibiting the abolition of the African slave trade for twenty years, that trade is spoken of as "The migration or importation of such persons as any of the States NOW EXISTING, shall think proper to admit," &c. These are the only provisions alluding to slavery. Thus, the thing is hid away, in the constitution, just as an afflicted man hides away a wen or a cancer, which he dares not cut out at once, lest he bleed to death; with the promise, nevertheless, that the cutting may begin at the end of a given time. Less than this our fathers COULD not do; and NOW [MORE?] they WOULD not do. Necessity drove them so far, and farther, they would not go. But this is not all. The earliest Congress, under the constitution, took the same view of slavery. They hedged and hemmed it in to the narrowest limits of necessity.

In 1794, they prohibited an out-going slave-trade---that is, the taking of slaves FROM the United States to sell.

In 1798, they prohibited the bringing of slaves from Africa, INTO the Mississippi Territory---this territory then comprising what are now the States of Mississippi and Alabama. This was TEN YEARS before they had the authority to do the same thing as to the States existing at the adoption of the constitution.

In 1800 they prohibited AMERICAN CITIZENS from trading in slaves between foreign countries---as, for instance, from Africa to Brazil.

In 1803 they passed a law in aid of one or two State laws, in restraint of the internal slave trade.

In 1807, in apparent hot haste, they passed the law, nearly a year in advance to take effect the first day of 1808---the very first day the constitution would permit---prohibiting the African slave trade by heavy pecuniary and corporal penalties.

In 1820, finding these provisions ineffectual, they declared the trade piracy, and annexed to it, the extreme penalty of death. While all this was passing in the general government, five or six of the original slave States had adopted systems of gradual emancipation; and by which the institution was rapidly becoming extinct within these limits.

Thus we see, the plain unmistakable spirit of that age, towards slavery, was hostility to the PRINCIPLE, and toleration, ONLY BY NECESSITY.

But NOW it is to be transformed into a "sacred right." Nebraska brings it forth, places it on the high road to extension and perpetuity; and, with a pat on its back, says to it, "Go, and God speed you." Henceforth it is to be the chief jewel of the nation---the very figure-head of the ship of State. Little by little, but steadily as man's march to the grave, we have been giving up the OLD for the NEW faith. Near eighty years ago we began by declaring that all men are created equal; but now from that beginning we have run down to the other declaration, that for SOME men to enslave OTHERS is a "sacred right of self-government." These principles can not stand together. They are as opposite as God and mammon; and whoever holds to the one, must despise the other. When Pettit, in connection with his support of the Nebraska bill, called the Declaration of Independence "a self-evident lie" he only did what consistency and candor require all other Nebraska men to do. Of the forty odd Nebraska Senators who sat present and heard him, no one rebuked him. Nor am I apprized that any Nebraska newspaper, or any Nebraska orator, in the whole nation, has ever yet rebuked him. If this had been said among Marion's men, Southerners though they were, what would have become of the man who said it? If this had been said to the men who captured Andre, the man who said it, would probably have been hung sooner than Andre was. If it had been said in old Independence Hall, seventy-eight years ago, the very door-keeper would have throttled the man, and thrust him into the street.

Let no one be deceived. The spirit of seventy-six and the spirit of Nebraska, are utter antagonisms; and the former is being rapidly displaced by the latter.

Fellow countrymen---Americans south, as well as north, shall we make no effort to arrest this? Already the liberal party throughout the world, express the apprehension "that the one retrograde institution in America, is undermining the principles of progress, and fatally violating the noblest political system the world ever saw." This is not the taunt of enemies, but the warning of friends. Is it quite safe to disregard it---to despise it? Is there no danger to liberty itself, in discarding the earliest practice, and first precept of our ancient faith? In our greedy chase to make profit of the negro, let us beware, lest we "cancel and tear to pieces" even the white man's charter of freedom.

Our republican robe is soiled, and trailed in the dust. Let us repurify it. Let us turn and wash it white, in the spirit, if not the blood, of the Revolution. Let us turn slavery from its claims of "moral right," back upon its existing legal rights, and its arguments of "necessity." Let us return it to the position our fathers gave it; and there let it rest in peace. Let us re-adopt the Declaration of Independence, and with it, the practices, and policy, which harmonize with it. Let north and south---let all Americans---let all lovers of liberty everywhere---join in the great and good work. If we do this, we shall not only have saved the Union; but we shall have so saved it, as to make, and to keep it, forever worthy of the saving. We shall have so saved it, that the succeeding millions of free happy people, the world over, shall rise up, and call us blessed, to the latest generations. . . .

To George Robertson, August 15, 1855

Hon: Geo. Robertson Springfield, Ills.
Lexington, Ky. Aug. 15. 1855

My dear Sir: The volume you left for me has been received. I am really grateful for the honor of your kind remembrance, as well as for the book. The partial reading I have already given it, has afforded me much of both pleasure and instruction. It was new to me that the exact question which led to the Missouri compromise, had arisen before it arose in regard to Missouri; and that you had taken so prominent a part in it. Your short, but able and patriotic speech upon that occasion, has not been improved upon since, by those holding the same views; and, with all the lights you then had, the views you took appear to me as very reasonable.

You are not a friend of slavery in the abstract. In that speech you spoke of "the peaceful extinction of slavery" and used other expressions indicating your belief that the thing was, at some time, to have an end[.] Since then we have had thirty six years of experience; and this experience has demonstrated, I think, that there is no peaceful extinction of slavery in prospect for us. The signal failure of Henry Clay, and other good and great men, in 1849, to effect any thing in favor of gradual emancipation in Kentucky, together with a thousand other signs, extinguishes that hope utterly. On the question of liberty, as a principle, we are not what we have been. When we were the political slaves of King George, and wanted to be free, we called the maxim that "all men are created equal" a self evident truth; but now when we have grown fat, and have lost all dread of being slaves ourselves, we have become so greedy to be masters that we call the same maxim "a self-evident lie" The fourth of July has not quite dwindled away; it is still a great day---for burning fire-crackers!!!

That spirit which desired the peaceful extinction of slavery, has itself become extinct, with the occasion, and the men of the Revolution. Under the impulse of that occasion, nearly half the states adopted systems of emancipation at once; and it is a significant fact, that not a single state has done the like since. So far as peaceful, voluntary emancipation is concerned, the condition of the negro slave in America, scarcely less terrible to the contemplation of a free mind, is now as fixed, and hopeless of change for the better, as that of the lost souls of the finally impenitent. The Autocrat of all the Russias will resign his crown, and proclaim his subjects free republicans sooner than will our American masters voluntarily give up their slaves.

Our political problem now is "Can we, as a nation, continue together permanently---forever---half slave, and half free?" The problem is too mighty for me. May God, in his mercy, superintend the solution. Your much obliged friend, and humble servant

A. LINCOLN---

From *Collected Works*. Abraham Lincoln Association, Springfield, IL. Roy P. Basler, editor; Marion Dolores Pratt and Lloyd A. Dunlap, assistant editors. Lincoln, Abraham, 1809-1865. New Brunswick, N.J.: Rutgers University Press, 1953. Copyright © The Abraham Lincoln Association. Reprinted by permission.

"A House Divided": Speech at Springfield, Illinois, June 16, 1858

(As printed in the Illinois State Journal, June 18, 1858, and the Chicago Daily Tribune, June 19, 1858)

Mr. PRESIDENT and Gentlemen of the Convention.

If we could first know where we are, and whither we are tending, we could then better judge what to do, and how to do it.

We are now far into the fifth year, since a policy was initiated, with the avowed object, and confident promise, of putting an end to slavery agitation.

Under the operation of that policy, that agitation has not only, not ceased, but has constantly augmented.

In my opinion, it will not cease, until a crisis shall have been reached, and passed.

"A house divided against itself cannot stand."

I believe this government cannot endure, permanently half slave and half free.

I do not expect the Union to be dissolved---I do not expect the house to fall---but I do expect it will cease to be divided.

It will become all one thing, or all the other.

Either the opponents of slavery, will arrest the further spread of it, and place it where the public mind shall rest in the belief that it is in course of ultimate extinction; or its advocates will push it forward, till it shall become alike lawful in all the States, old as well as new---North as well as South.

Have we no tendency to the latter condition?

Let any one who doubts, carefully contemplate that now almost complete legal combination---piece of machinery so to speak---compounded of the Nebraska doctrine, and the Dred Scott decision. Let him consider not only what work the machinery is adapted to do, and how well adapted; but also, let him study the history of its construction, and trace, if he can, or rather fail, if he can, to trace the evidences of design, and concert of action, among its chief bosses, from the beginning.

But, so far, Congress only, had acted; and an indorsement by the people, real or apparent, was indispensable, to save the point already gained, and give chance for more.

The new year of 1854 found slavery excluded from more than half the States by State Constitutions, and from most of the national territory by Congressional prohibition.

Four days later, commenced the struggle, which ended in repealing that Congressional prohibition.

This opened all the national territory to slavery; and was the first point gained.

This necessity had not been overlooked; but had been provided for, as well as might be, in the notable argument of "squatter sovereignty," otherwise called "sacred right of self government," which latter phrase, though expressive of the only rightful basis of any government, was so perverted in this attempted use of it as to amount to just this: That if any one man, choose to enslave another, no third man shall be allowed to object.

That argument was incorporated into the Nebraska bill itself, in the language which follows: "It being the true intent and meaning of this act not to legislate slavery into any Territory or state, nor to exclude it therefrom; but to leave the people thereof perfectly free to form and regulate their domestic institutions in their own way, subject only to the Constitution of the United States."

Then opened the roar of loose declamation in favor of "Squatter Sovereignty," and "Sacred right of self government."

"But," said opposition members, "let us be more specific---let us amend the bill so as to expressly declare that the people of the territory may exclude slavery." "Not we," said the friends of the measure; and down they voted the amendment.

While the Nebraska bill was passing through congress, a law case, involving the question of a negroe's freedom, by reason of his owner having voluntarily taken him first into a free state and then a territory covered by the congressional prohibition, and held him as a slave, for a long time in each, was passing through the U.S. Circuit Court for the District of Missouri; and both Nebraska bill and law suit were brought to a decision in the same month of May, 1854. The negroe's name was "Dred Scott," which name now designates the decision finally made in the case.

Before the then next Presidential election, the law case came to, and was argued in the Supreme Court of the United States; but the decision of it was deferred until after the election. Still, before the election, Senator Trumbull, on the floor of the Senate, requests the leading advocate of the Nebraska bill to state his opinion whether the people of a territory can constitutionally exclude slavery from their limits; and the latter answers, "That is a question for the Supreme Court."

The election came. Mr. Buchanan was elected, and the indorsement, such as it was, secured. That was the second point gained. The indorsement, however, fell short of a clear popular majority by nearly four hundred thousand votes, and so, perhaps, was not overwhelmingly reliable and satisfactory.

The outgoing President, in his last annual message, as impressively as possible echoed back upon the people the weight and authority of the indorsement.

The Supreme Court met again; did not announce their decision, but ordered a re-argument.

The Presidential inauguration came, and still no decision of the court; but the incoming President, in his inaugural address, fervently exhorted the people to abide by the forthcoming decision, whatever it might be.

Then, in a few days, came the decision.

The reputed author of the Nebraska bill finds an early occasion to make a speech at this capitol indorsing the Dred Scott Decision, and vehemently denouncing all opposition to it.

The new President, too, seizes the early occasion of the Silliman letter to indorse and strongly construe that decision, and to express his astonishment that any different view had ever been entertained.

At length a squabble springs up between the President and the author of the Nebraska bill, on the mere question of fact, whether the Lecompton constitution was or was not, in any just sense, made by the people of Kansas; and in that squabble the latter declares that all he wants is a fair vote for the people, and that he cares not whether slavery be voted down or voted up. I do not understand his declaration that he cares not whether slavery be voted down or voted up, to be intended by him other than as an apt definition of the policy he would impress upon the public mind---the principle for which he declares he has suffered much, and is ready to suffer to the end.

And well may he cling to that principle. If he has any parental feeling, well may he cling to it. That principle, is the only shred left of his original Nebraska doctrine. Under the Dred Scott decision, "squatter sovereignty" squatted out of existence, tumbled down like temporary scaffolding---like the mould at the foundry served through one blast and fell back into loose sand---helped to carry an election, and then was kicked to the winds. His late joint struggle with the Republicans, against the Lecompton Constitution, involves nothing of the original Nebraska doctrine. That struggle was made on a point, the right of a people to make their own constitution, upon which he and the Republicans have never differed.

The several points of the Dred Scott decision, in connection with Senator Douglas' "care not" policy, constitute the piece of machinery, in its present state of advancement. This was the third point gained.

The working points of that machinery are:

First, that no negro slave, imported as such from Africa, and no descendant of such slave can ever be a citizen of any State, in the sense of that term as used in the Constitution of the United States.

This point is made in order to deprive the negro, in every possible event, of the benefit of this provision of the United States Constitution, which declares that---

"The citizens of each State shall be entitled to all privileges and immunities of citizens in the several States."

Secondly, that "subject to the Constitution of the United States," neither Congress nor a Territorial Legislature can exclude slavery from any United States territory.

This point is made in order that individual men may fill up the territories with slaves, without danger of losing them as property, and thus to enhance the chances of permanency to the institution through all the future.

Thirdly, that whether the holding a negro in actual slavery in a free State, makes him free, as against the holder, the United States courts will not decide, but will leave to be decided by the courts of any slave State the negro may be forced into by the master.

This point is made, not to be pressed immediately; but, if acquiesced in for a while, and apparently indorsed by the people at an election, then to sustain the logical conclusion that what Dred Scott's master might lawfully do with Dred Scott, in the free State of Illinois, every other master may lawfully do with any other one, or one thousand slaves, in Illinois, or in any other free State.

Auxiliary to all this, and working hand in hand with it, the Nebraska doctrine, or what is left of it, is to educate and mould public opinion, at least Northern public opinion, to not care whether slavery is voted down or voted up.

This shows exactly where we now are; and partially also, whither we are tending.

It will throw additional light on the latter, to go back, and run the mind over the string of historical facts already stated. Several things will now appear less dark and mysterious than they did when they were transpiring. The people were to be left "perfectly free" "subject only to the Constitution." What the Constitution had to do with it, outsiders could not then see. Plainly enough now, it was an exactly fitted niche, for the Dred Scott decision to afterwards come in, and declare the perfect freedom of the people, to be just no freedom at all.

Why was the amendment, expressly declaring the right of the people to exclude slavery, voted down? Plainly enough now, the adoption of it, would have spoiled the niche for the Dred Scott decision.

Why was the court decision held up? Why, even a Senator's individual opinion withheld, till after the Presidential election? Plainly enough now, the speaking out then would have damaged the "perfectly free" argument upon which the election was to be carried.

Why the outgoing President's felicitation on the indorsement? Why the delay of a reargument? Why the incoming President's advance exhortation in favor of the decision?

These things look like the cautious patting and petting a spirited horse, preparatory to mounting him, when it is dreaded that he may give the rider a fall.

And why the hasty after indorsements of the decision by the President and others?

We can not absolutely know that all these exact adaptations are the result of preconcert. But when we see a lot of framed timbers, different portions of which we know have been gotten out at different times and places and by different workmen---Stephen, Franklin, Roger and James, for instance---and when we see these timbers joined together, and see they exactly make the frame of a house or a mill, all the tenons and mortices exactly fitting, and all the lengths and proportions of the different pieces exactly adapted to their respective places, and not a piece too many or too few---not omitting even scaffolding---or, if a single piece be lacking, we can see the place in the frame exactly fitted and prepared to yet bring such piece in---in such a case, we find it impossible to not believe that Stephen and Franklin and Roger and James all understood one another from the beginning, and all worked upon a common plan or draft drawn up before the first lick was struck.

It should not be overlooked that, by the Nebraska bill, the people of a State as well as Territory, were to be left "perfectly free" "subject only to the Constitution."

Why mention a State? They were legislating for territories, and not for or about States. Certainly the people of a State are and ought to be subject to the Constitution of the United States; but why is mention of this lugged into this merely territorial law? Why are the people of a territory and the people of a state therein lumped together, and their relation to the Constitution therein treated as being precisely the same?

While the opinion of the Court, by Chief Justice Taney, in the Dred Scott case, and the separate opinions of all the concurring Judges, expressly declare that the Constitution of the United States neither permits Congress nor a Territorial legislature to exclude slavery from any United States territory, they all omit to declare whether or not the same Constitution permits a state, or the people of a State, to exclude it.

Possibly, this was a mere omission; but who can be quite sure, if McLean or Curtis had sought to get into the opinion a declaration of unlimited power in the people of a state to exclude slavery from their limits, just as Chase and Macy sought to get such declaration, in behalf of the people of a territory, into the Nebraska bill---I ask, who can be quite sure that it would not have been voted down, in the one case, as it had been in the other.

The nearest approach to the point of declaring the power of a State over slavery, is made by Judge Nelson. He approaches it more than once, using the precise idea, and almost the language too, of the Nebraska act. On one occasion his exact language is, "except in cases where the power is restrained by the Constitution of the United States, the law of the State is supreme over the subject of slavery within its jurisdiction."

In what cases the power of the states is so restrained by the U.S. Constitution, is left an open question, precisely as the same question, as to the restraint on the power of the territories was left open in the Nebraska act. Put that and that together, and we have another nice little niche, which we may, ere long, see filled with another Supreme Court decision, declaring that the Constitution of the United States does not permit a state to exclude slavery from its limits.

And this may especially be expected if the doctrine of "care not whether slavery be voted down or voted up," shall gain upon the public mind sufficiently to give promise that such a decision can be maintained when made.

Such a decision is all that slavery now lacks of being alike lawful in all the States.

Welcome or unwelcome, such decision is probably coming, and will soon be upon us, unless the power of the present political dynasty shall be met and overthrown.

We shall lie down pleasantly dreaming that the people of Missouri are on the verge of making their State free; and we shall awake to the reality, instead, that the Supreme Court has made Illinois a slave State.

To meet and overthrow the power of that dynasty, is the work now before all those who would prevent that consummation.

That is what we have to do.

But how can we best do it?

There are those who denounce us openly to their own friends, and yet whisper us softly, that Senator Douglas is the aptest instrument there is, with which to effect that object. They do not tell us, nor has he told us, that he wishes any such object to be effected. They wish us to infer all, from the facts, that he now has a little quarrel with the present head of the dynasty; and that he has regularly voted with us, on a single point, upon which, he and we, have never differed.

They remind us that he is a very great man, and that the largest of us are very small ones. Let this be granted. But "a living dog is better than a dead lion." Judge Douglas, if not a dead lion for this work, is at least a caged and toothless one. How can he oppose the advances of slavery? He don't care anything about it. His avowed mission is impressing the "public heart" to care nothing about it.

A leading Douglas Democratic newspaper thinks Douglas' superior talent will be needed to resist the revival of the African slave trade.

Does Douglas believe an effort to revive that trade is approaching? He has not said so. Does he really think so? But if it is, how can he resist it? For years he has labored to prove it a sacred right of white men to take negro slaves into the new territories. Can he possibly show that it is less a sacred right to buy them where they can be bought cheapest? And, unquestionably they can be bought cheaper in Africa than in Virginia.

He has done all in his power to reduce the whole question of slavery to one of a mere right of property; and as such, how can he oppose the foreign slave trade---

how can he refuse that trade in that "property" shall be "perfectly free"---unless he does it as a protection to the home production? And as the home producers will probably not ask the protection, he will be wholly without a ground of opposition.

Senator Douglas holds, we know, that a man may rightfully be wiser to-day than he was yesterday---that he may rightfully change when he finds himself wrong.

But, can we for that reason, run ahead, and infer that he will make any particular change, of which he, himself, has given no intimation? Can we safely base our action upon any such vague inference?

Now, as ever, I wish to not misrepresent Judge Douglas' position, question his motives, or do ought that can be personally offensive to him.

Whenever, if ever, he and we can come together on principle so that our great cause may have assistance from his great ability, I hope to have interposed no adventitious obstacle.

But clearly, he is not now with us---he does not pretend to be---he does not promise to ever be.

Our cause, then, must be intrusted to, and conducted by its own undoubted friends---those whose hands are free, whose hearts are in the work---who do care for the result.

Two years ago the Republicans of the nation mustered over thirteen hundred thousand strong.

We did this under the single impulse of resistance to a common danger, with every external circumstance against us.

Of strange, discordant, and even, hostile elements, we gathered from the four winds, and formed and fought the battle through, under the constant hot fire of a disciplined, proud, and pampered enemy.

Did we brave all then, to falter now?---now---when that same enemy is wavering, dissevered and belligerent?

The result is not doubtful. We shall not fail---if we stand firm, we shall not fail. Wise councils may accelerate or mistakes delay it, but, sooner or later the victory is sure to come.

Fourth Debate with Stephen A. Douglas at Charleston, Illinois, September 18, 1858

LADIES AND GENTLEMEN: It will be very difficult for an audience so large as this to hear distinctly what a speaker says, and consequently it is important that as profound silence be preserved as possible.

While I was at the hotel to-day an elderly gentleman called upon me to know whether I was really in favor of producing a perfect equality between the negroes and white people. [Great laughter.] While I had not proposed to myself on this occasion to say much on that subject, yet as the question was asked me I thought I would occupy perhaps five minutes in saying something in regard to it. I will say then that I am not, nor ever have been in favor of bringing about in any way the social and political equality of the white and black races, [applause]---that I am not nor ever have been in favor of making voters or jurors of negroes, nor of qualifying them to hold office, nor to intermarry with white people; and I will say in addition to this that there is a physical difference between the white and black races which I believe will for ever forbid the two races living together on terms of social and political equality. And inasmuch as they cannot so live, while they do remain together there must be the position of superior and inferior, and I as much as any other man am in favor of having the superior position assigned to the white race. I say upon this occasion I do not perceive that because the white man is to have the superior position the negro should be denied everything. I do not understand that because I do not want a negro woman for a slave I must necessarily want her for a wife. [Cheers and laughter.] My understanding is that I can just let her alone. I am now in my fiftieth year, and I certainly never have had a black woman for either a slave or a wife. So it seems to me quite possible for us to get along without making either slaves or wives of negroes. I will add to this that I have never seen to my knowledge a man, woman or child who was in favor of producing a perfect equality, social and political, between negroes and white men. I recollect of but one distinguished instance that I ever heard of so frequently as to be entirely satisfied of its correctness---and that is the case of Judge Douglas' old friend Col. Richard M. Johnson. [Laughter.] I will also add to the remarks I have made, (for I am not going to enter at large upon this subject,) that I have never had the least apprehension that I or my friends would marry negroes if there was no law to keep them from it, [laughter] but as Judge Douglas and his friends seem to be in great apprehension that they might, if there were no law to keep them from it, [roars of laughter] I give him the most solemn pledge that I will to the very last stand by the law of this State, which forbids the marrying of white people with negroes. [Continued laughter and applause.] I will add one further word, which is this, that I do not understand there is any place where an alteration of the social and political relations of the negro and the white man can be made except in the State Legislature---not in the Congress of the United States---and as I do not really apprehend the approach of any such thing myself, and as Judge Douglas seems to be in constant horror that some such danger is rapidly approaching, I propose as the best means to prevent it that the Judge be kept at home and placed in the State Legislature to fight the measure. [Uproarious laughter and applause.] I do not propose dwelling longer at this time on this subject. . . .

. . . Judge Douglas has said to you that he has not been able to get from me an answer to the question whether I am in favor of negro-citizenship. So far as I know, the Judge never asked me the question before. [Applause.] He shall have no occasion to ever ask it again, for I tell him very frankly that I am not in favor of negro citizenship. [Renewed applause.] This furnishes me an occasion for saying a few words upon the subject. I mentioned in a certain speech of mine which has been printed, that the Supreme Court had decided that a negro could not possibly be made a citizen, and without saying what was my ground of complaint in regard to that, or whether I had any ground of complaint, Judge Douglas has from that thing manufactured nearly every thing that he ever says about my disposition to produce an equality between the negroes and the white people. [Laughter and applause.] If any one will read my speech, he will find I mentioned that as one of the points decided in the course of the Supreme Court opinions, but I did not state what objection I had to it. But Judge Douglas tells the people what my objection was when I did not tell them myself. [Loud applause and laughter.] Now my opinion is that the different States have the power to make a negro a citizen under the Constitution of the United States if they choose. The Dred Scott decision decides that they have not that power. If the State of Illinois had that power I should be opposed to the exercise of it. [Cries of "good," "good," and applause.] That is all I have to say about it.

Judge Douglas has told me that he heard my speeches north and my speeches south---that he had heard me at Ottawa and at Freeport in the north, and recently at Jonesboro in the south, and there was a very different cast of sentiment in the speeches made at the different points. I will not charge upon Judge Douglas that he wilfully misrepresents me, but I call upon every fair-minded man to take these speeches and read them, and I dare him to point out any difference between my printed speeches north and south. [Great cheering.] While I am here perhaps I ought to say a word, if I have the time, in regard to the latter portion of the Judge's speech, which was a sort of declamation in reference to my having said I entertained the belief that this government would not endure, half slave and half free. I have said so and I did not say it without what seemed to me to be good reasons. It perhaps would require more time than I have now to set forth these reasons in detail; but let me ask you a few questions. Have we ever had any peace on this slavery question? [No, no.] When are we to have peace upon it if it is kept in the position it now occupies? [Never.] How are we ever to have peace upon it? That is an important question. To be sure if we will all stop and allow Judge Douglas and his friends to march on in their present career until they plant the institution all over the nation, here and wherever else our flag waves, and we acquiesce in it, there will be peace. But let me ask Judge Douglas how he is going to get the people to do that? [Applause.] They have been wrangling over this question for at least forty years. This was the cause of the agitation resulting in the Missouri Compromise---this produced the troubles at the annexation of Texas, in the acquisition of the territory acquired in the Mexican war. Again, this was the trouble which was quieted by the Compromise of 1850, when it was settled "forever," as both the great political parties declared in their National Conventions. That "forever" turned out to be just four years, [laughter] when Judge Douglas himself re-opened it. [Immense applause, cries of "hit him again," &c.] When is it likely to come to an end? He introduced the Nebraska bill in 1854 to put another end to the slavery agitation. He promised that it would finish it all up immediately, and he has never made a speech since until he got into a quarrel with the President about the Lecompton Constitution, in which he has not declared that we are just at the end of the slavery agitation. But in one speech, I think last winter, he did say that he didn't quite see when the end of the slavery agitation would come. [Laughter and cheers.] Now he tells us again that it is all over, and the people of Kansas have voted down the Lecompton Constitution. How is it over? That was only one of the attempts at putting an end to the slavery agitation---one of these "final settlements." [Renewed laughter.] Is Kansas in the Union? Has she formed a Constitution that she is likely to come in under? Is not the slavery agitation still an open question in that Territory? Has the voting down of that Constitution put an end to all the trouble? Is that more likely to settle it than every one of these previous attempts to settle the slavery agitation. [Cries of "No," "No."] Now, at this day in the history of the world we can no more foretell where the end of this slavery agitation will be than we can see the end of the world itself. The Nebraska-Kansas bill was introduced four years and a half ago, and if the agitation is ever to come to an end, we may say we are four years and a half nearer the end. So, too, we can say we are four years and a half nearer the end of the world; and we can just as clearly see the end of the world as we can see the end of this agitation. [Applause.] The Kansas settlement did not conclude it. If Kansas should sink to-day, and leave a great vacant space in the earth's surface, this vexed question would still be among us. I say, then, there is no way of putting an end to the slavery agitation amongst us but to put it back upon the basis where our fathers placed it, [applause] no way but to keep it out of our new Territories [renewed applause]---to restrict it forever to the old States where it now exists. [Tremendous and prolonged cheering; cries of "That's the doctrine," "Good," "Good," &c.] Then the public mind will rest in the belief that it is in the course of ultimate extinction. That is one way of putting an end to the slavery agitation. [Applause.]

The other way is for us to surrender and let Judge Douglas and his friends have their way and plant slavery over all the States---cease speaking of it as in any way a wrong---regard slavery as one of the common matters of property, and speak of negroes as we do of our horses and cattle. But while it drives on in its state of progress as it is now driving, and as it has driven for the last five years, I have ventured the opinion, and I say to-day, that we will have no end to the slavery agitation until it takes one turn or the other. [Applause.] I do not mean that when it takes a turn towards ultimate extinction it will be in a day, nor in a year, nor in two years. I do not suppose that in the most peaceful way ultimate extinction would occur in less than a hundred years at the least; but that it will occur in the best way for both races in God's own good time, I have no doubt. [Applause.] But, my friends, I have used up more of my time than I intended on this point.

From *Collected Works*. Abraham Lincoln Association, Springfield, IL. Roy P. Basler, editor; Marion Dolores Pratt and Lloyd A. Dunlap, assistant editors. Lincoln, Abraham, 1809-1865. New Brunswick, N.J.: Rutgers University Press, 1953. Copyright © The Abraham Lincoln Association. Reprinted by permission.

ABRAHAM LINCOLN, TAKEN ON THE DAY OF THE ADDRESS AT COOPER INSTITUTE

New York City, February 27, 1860

MR. PRESIDENT AND FELLOW-CITIZENS OF NEW-YORK:---The facts with which I shall deal this evening are mainly old and familiar; nor is there anything new in the general use I shall make of them. If there shall be any novelty, it will be in the mode of presenting the facts, and the inferences and observations following that presentation.

In his speech last autumn, at Columbus, Ohio, as reported in "The New-York Times," Senator Douglas said:

"Our fathers, when they framed the Government under which we live, understood this question just as well, and even better, than we do now."

I fully indorse this, and I adopt it as a text for this discourse. I so adopt it because it furnishes a precise and an agreed starting point for a discussion between Republicans and that wing of the Democracy headed by Senator Douglas. It simply leaves the inquiry: "What was the understanding those fathers had of the question mentioned?"

What is the frame of Government under which we live?

The answer must be: "The Constitution of the United States." That Constitution consists of the original, framed in 1787, (and under which the present government first went into operation,) and twelve subsequently framed amendments, the first ten of which were framed in 1789.

Who were our fathers that framed the Constitution? I suppose the "thirty-nine" who signed the original instrument may be fairly called our fathers who framed that part of the present Government. It is almost exactly true to say they framed it, and it is altogether true to say they fairly represented the opinion and sentiment of the whole nation at that time. Their names, being familiar to nearly all, and accessible to quite all, need not now be repeated.

I take these "thirty-nine" for the present, as being "our fathers who framed the Government under which we live."

What is the question which, according to the text, those fathers understood "just as well, and even better than we do now?"

It is this: Does the proper division of local from federal authority, or anything in the Constitution, forbid our Federal Government to control as to slavery in our Federal Territories?

Upon this, Senator Douglas holds the affirmative, and Republicans the negative. This affirmation and denial form an issue; and this issue---this question---is precisely what the text declares our fathers understood "better than we." . . .

. . . If any man at this day sincerely believes that a proper division of local from federal authority, or any part of the Constitution, forbids the Federal Government to control as to slavery in the federal territories, he is right to say so, and to enforce his position by all truthful evidence and fair argument which he can. But he has no right to mislead others, who have less access to history, and less leisure to study it, into the false belief that "our fathers, who framed the Government under which we live," were of the same opinion---thus substituting falsehood and deception for truthful evidence and fair argument. If any man at this day sincerely believes "our fathers who framed the Government under which we live," used and applied principles, in other cases, which ought to have led them to understand that a proper division of local from federal authority or some part of the Constitution, forbids the Federal Government to control as to slavery in the federal territories, he is right to say so. But he should, at the same time, brave the responsibility of declaring that, in his opinion, he understands their principles better than they did themselves; and especially should he not shirk that responsibility by asserting that they "understood the question just as well, and even better, than we do now."

But enough! Let all who believe that "our fathers, who framed the Government under which we live, understood this question just as well, and even better, than we do now," speak as they spoke, and act as they acted upon it. This is all Republicans ask---all Republicans desire---in relation to slavery. As those fathers marked it, so let it be again marked, as an evil not to be extended, but to be tolerated and protected only because of and so far as its actual presence among us makes that toleration and protection a necessity. Let all the guaranties those fathers gave it, be, not grudgingly, but fully and fairly maintained. For this Republicans contend, and with this, so far as I know or believe, they will be content. And now, if they would listen---as I suppose they will not---I would address a few words to the Southern people.

I would say to them:---You consider yourselves a reasonable and a just people; and I consider that in the general qualities of reason and justice you are not inferior to any other people. Still, when you speak of us Republicans, you do so only to denounce us as reptiles, or, at the best, as no better than outlaws. You will grant a hearing to pirates or murderers, but nothing like it to "Black Republicans." In all your contentions with one another, each of you deems an unconditional condemnation of "Black Republicanism" as the first thing to be attended to. Indeed, such condemnation of us seems to be an indispensable prerequisite---license, so to speak---among you to be admitted or permitted to speak at all. Now, can you, or not, be prevailed upon to pause and to consider whether this is quite just to us, or even to yourselves? Bring forward your charges and specifications, and then be patient long enough to hear us deny or justify.

You say we are sectional. We deny it. That makes an issue; and the burden of proof is upon you. You produce your proof; and what is it? Why, that our party has no existence in your section---gets no votes in your section. The fact is substantially true; but does it prove the issue? If it does, then in case we should, without change of principle, begin to get votes in your section, we should thereby cease to be sectional. You cannot escape this conclusion; and yet, are you willing to abide by it? If you are, you will probably soon find that we have ceased to be sectional, for we shall get votes in your section this very year. You will then begin to discover, as the truth plainly is, that your proof does not touch the issue. The fact that we get no votes in your section, is a fact of your making, and not of ours. And if there be fault in that fact, that fault is primarily yours, and remains so until you show that we repel you by some wrong principle or practice. If we do repel you by any wrong principle or practice, the fault is ours; but this brings you to where you ought to have started---to a discussion of the right or wrong of our principle. If our principle, put in practice, would wrong your section for the benefit of ours, or for any other object, then our principle, and we with it, are sectional, and are justly opposed and denounced as such. Meet us, then, on the question of whether our principle, put in practice, would wrong your section; and so meet us as if it were possible that something may be said on our side. Do you accept the challenge? No! Then you really believe that the principle which "our fathers who framed the Government under which we live" thought so clearly right as to adopt it, and indorse it again and again, upon their official oaths, is in fact so clearly wrong as to demand your condemnation without a moment's consideration.

Some of you delight to flaunt in our faces the warning against sectional parties given by Washington in his Farewell Address. Less than eight years before Washington gave that warning, he had, as President of the United States, approved and signed an act of Congress, enforcing the prohibition of slavery in the North-western Territory, which act embodied the policy of the Government upon that subject up to and at the very moment he penned that warning; and about one year after he penned it, he wrote La Fayette that he considered that prohibition a wise measure, expressing in the same connection his hope that we should at some time have a confederacy of free States.

Bearing this in mind, and seeing that sectionalism has since arisen upon this same subject, is that warning a weapon in your hands against us, or in our hands against you? Could Washington himself speak, would he cast the blame of that sectionalism upon us, who sustain his policy, or upon you who repudiate it? We respect that warning of Washington, and we commend it to you, together with his example pointing to the right application of it.

But you say you are conservative---eminently conservative---while we are revolutionary, destructive, or something of the sort. What is conservatism? Is it not adherence to the old and tried, against the new and untried? We stick to, contend for, the identical old policy on the point in controversy which was adopted by "our fathers who framed the Government under which we live;" while you with one accord reject, and scout, and spit upon that old policy, and insist upon substituting something new. True, you disagree among yourselves as to what that substitute shall be. You are divided on new propositions and plans, but you are unanimous in rejecting and denouncing the old policy of the fathers. Some of you are for reviving the foreign slave trade; some for a Congressional

Slave-Code for the Territories; some for Congress forbidding the Territories to prohibit Slavery within their limits; some for maintaining Slavery in the Territories through the judiciary; some for the "gur-reat pur-rinciple" that "if one man would enslave another, no third man should object," fantastically called "Popular Sovereignty;" but never a man among you in favor of federal prohibition of slavery in federal territories, according to the practice of "our fathers who framed the Government under which we live." Not one of all your various plans can show a precedent or an advocate in the century within which our Government originated. Consider, then, whether your claim of conservatism for yourselves, and your charge of destructiveness against us, are based on the most clear and stable foundations.

Again, you say we have made the slavery question more prominent than it formerly was. We deny it. We admit that it is more prominent, but we deny that we made it so. It was not we, but you, who discarded the old policy of the fathers. We resisted, and still resist, your innovation; and thence comes the greater prominence of the question. Would you have that question reduced to its former proportions? Go back to that old policy. What has been will be again, under the same conditions. If you would have the peace of the old times, readopt the precepts and policy of the old times.

You charge that we stir up insurrections among your slaves. We deny it; and what is your proof? Harper's Ferry! John Brown!! John Brown was no Republican; and you have failed to implicate a single Republican in his Harper's Ferry enterprise. If any member of our party is guilty in that matter, you know it or you do not know it. If you do know it, you are inexcusable for not designating the man and proving the fact. If you do not know it, you are inexcusable for asserting it, and especially for persisting in the assertion after you have tried and failed to make the proof. You need not be told that persisting in a charge which one does not know to be true, is simply malicious slander.

Some of you admit that no Republican designedly aided or encouraged the Harper's Ferry affair; but still insist that our doctrines and declarations necessarily lead to such results. We do not believe it. We know we hold to no doctrine, and make no declaration, which were not held to and made by "our fathers who framed the Government under which we live." You never dealt fairly by us in relation to this affair. When it occurred, some important State elections were near at hand, and you were in evident glee with the belief that, by charging the blame upon us, you could get an advantage of us in those elections. The elections came, and your expectations were not quite fulfilled. Every Republican man knew that, as to himself at least, your charge was a slander, and he was not much inclined by it to cast his vote in your favor. Republican doctrines and declarations are accompanied with a continual protest against any interference whatever with your slaves, or with you about your slaves. Surely, this does not encourage them to revolt. True, we do, in common with "our fathers, who framed the Government under which we live," declare our belief that slavery is wrong; but the slaves do not hear us declare even this. For anything we say or do, the slaves would scarcely know there is a Republican party. I believe they would not, in fact, generally know it but for your misrepresentations of us, in their hearing. In your political contests among yourselves, each faction charges the other with sympathy with Black Republicanism; and then, to give point to the charge, defines Black Republicanism to simply be insurrection, blood and thunder among the slaves.

Slave insurrections are no more common now than they were before the Republican party was organized. What induced the Southampton insurrection, twenty-eight years ago, in which, at least, three times as many lives were lost as at Harper's Ferry? You can scarcely stretch your very elastic fancy to the conclusion that Southampton was "got up by Black Republicanism." In the present state of things in the United States, I do not think a general, or even a very extensive slave insurrection, is possible. The indispensable concert of action cannot be attained. The slaves have no means of rapid communication; nor can incendiary freemen, black or white, supply it. The explosive materials are everywhere in parcels; but there neither are, nor can be supplied, the indispensable connecting trains.

Much is said by Southern people about the affection of slaves for their masters and mistresses; and a part of it, at least, is true. A plot for an uprising could scarcely be devised and communicated to twenty individuals before some one of them, to save the life of a favorite master or mistress, would divulge it. This is the rule; and the slave revolution in Hayti was not an exception to it, but a case occurring under peculiar circumstances. The gunpowder plot of British history, though not connected with slaves, was more in point. In that case, only about twenty were admitted to the secret; and yet one of them, in his anxiety to save a friend, betrayed the plot to that friend, and, by consequence, averted the calamity. Occasional poisonings from the kitchen, and open or stealthy assassinations in the field, and local revolts extending to a score or so, will continue to occur as the natural results of slavery; but no general insurrection of slaves, as I think, can happen in this country for a long time. Whoever much fears, or much hopes for such an event, will be alike disappointed.

In the language of Mr. Jefferson, uttered many years ago, "It is still in our power to direct the process of emancipation, and deportation, peaceably, and in such slow degrees, as that the evil will wear off insensibly; and their places be, pari passu, filled up by free white laborers. If, on the contrary, it is left to force itself on, human nature must shudder at the prospect held up."

Mr. Jefferson did not mean to say, nor do I, that the power of emancipation is in the Federal Government. He spoke of Virginia; and, as to the power of emancipation, I speak of the slaveholding States only. The Federal Government, however, as we insist, has the power of restraining the extension of the institution---the power to insure that a slave insurrection shall never occur on any American soil which is now free from slavery.

John Brown's effort was peculiar. It was not a slave insurrection. It was an attempt by white men to get up a revolt among slaves, in which the slaves refused to participate. In fact, it was so absurd that the slaves, with all their ignorance, saw plainly enough it could not succeed. That affair, in its philosophy, corresponds with the many attempts, related in history, at the assassination of kings and emperors. An enthusiast broods over the oppression of a people till he fancies himself commissioned by Heaven to liberate them. He ventures the attempt, which ends in little else than his own execution. Orsini's attempt on Louis Napoleon, and John Brown's attempt at Harper's Ferry were, in their philosophy, precisely the same. The eagerness to cast blame on old England in the one case, and on New England in the other, does not disprove the sameness of the two things.

And how much would it avail you, if you could, by the use of John Brown, Helper's Book, and the like, break up the Republican organization? Human action can be modified to some extent, but human nature cannot be changed. There is a judgment and a feeling against slavery in this nation, which cast at least a million and a half of votes. You cannot destroy that judgment and feeling---that sentiment---by breaking up the political organization which rallies around it. You can scarcely scatter and disperse an army which has been formed into order in the face of your heaviest fire; but if you could, how much would you gain by forcing the sentiment which created it out of the peaceful channel of the ballot-box, into some other channel? What would that other channel probably be? Would the number of John Browns be lessened or enlarged by the operation?

But you will break up the Union rather than submit to a denial of your Constitutional rights.

That has a somewhat reckless sound; but it would be palliated, if not fully justified, were we proposing, by the mere force of numbers, to deprive you of some right, plainly written down in the Constitution. But we are proposing no such thing.

When you make these declarations, you have a specific and well-understood allusion to an assumed Constitutional right of yours, to take slaves into the federal territories, and to hold them there as property. But no such right is specifically written in the Constitution. That instrument is literally silent about any such right. We, on the contrary, deny that such a right has any existence in the Constitution, even by implication.

Your purpose, then, plainly stated, is, that you will destroy the Government, unless you be allowed to construe and enforce the Constitution as you please, on all points in dispute between you and us. You will rule or ruin in all events. This, plainly stated, is your language. Perhaps you will say the Supreme Court has decided the disputed Constitutional question in your favor. Not quite so. But waiving the lawyer's distinction between dictum and decision, the Court have decided the question for you in a sort of way. The Court have substantially said, it is your Constitutional right to take slaves into the federal territories, and to hold them there as property. When I say the decision was made in a sort of way, I mean it was made in a divided Court, by a bare majority of the Judges, and they not quite agreeing with one another in the reasons for making it; that it is so made as that its avowed supporters disagree with one another about its meaning, and that it was mainly based upon a mistaken statement of fact---the statement in the opinion that "the right of property in a slave is distinctly and expressly affirmed in the Constitution."

An inspection of the Constitution will show that the right of property in a slave is not "distinctly and expressly affirmed" in it. Bear in mind, the Judges do not pledge their judicial opinion that such right is impliedly affirmed in the Constitution; but they pledge their veracity that it is "distinctly and expressly" affirmed there---"distinctly," that is, not mingled with anything else---"expressly," that is, in words meaning just that, without the aid of any inference, and susceptible of no other meaning.

If they had only pledged their judicial opinion that such right is affirmed in the instrument by implication, it would be open to others to show that neither the word "slave" nor "slavery" is to be found in the Constitution, nor the word "property" even, in any connection with language alluding to the things slave, or slavery, and that wherever in that instrument the slave is alluded to, he is called a "person;"---and wherever his master's legal right in relation to him is alluded to, it is spoken of as "service or labor which may be due,"---as a debt payable in service or labor. Also, it would be open to show, by contemporaneous history, that this mode of alluding to slaves and slavery, instead of speaking of them, was employed on purpose to exclude from the Constitution the idea that there could be property in man.

To show all this, is easy and certain.

When this obvious mistake of the Judges shall be brought to their notice, is it not reasonable to expect that they will withdraw the mistaken statement, and reconsider the conclusion based upon it?

And then it is to be remembered that "our fathers, who framed the Government under which we live"---the men who made the Constitution---decided this same Constitutional question in our favor, long ago---decided it without division among themselves, when making the decision; without division among themselves about the meaning of it after it was made, and, so far as any evidence is left, without basing it upon any mistaken statement of facts.

Under all these circumstances, do you really feel yourselves justified to break up this Government, unless such a court decision as yours is, shall be at once submitted to as a conclusive and final rule of political action? But you will not abide the election of a Republican President! In that supposed event, you say, you will destroy the Union; and then, you say, the great crime of having destroyed it will be upon us! That is cool. A highwayman holds a pistol to my ear, and mutters through his teeth, "Stand and deliver, or I shall kill you, and then you will be a murderer!"

To be sure, what the robber demanded of me---my money---was my own; and I had a clear right to keep it; but it was no more my own than my vote is my own; and the threat of death to me, to extort my money, and the threat of destruction to the Union, to extort my vote, can scarcely be distinguished in principle.

A few words now to Republicans. It is exceedingly desirable that all parts of this great Confederacy shall be at peace, and in harmony, one with another. Let us Republicans do our part to have it so. Even though much provoked, let us do nothing through passion and ill temper. Even though the southern people will not so much as listen to us, let us calmly consider their demands, and yield to them if, in our deliberate view of our duty, we possibly can. Judging by all they say and do, and by the subject and nature of their controversy with us, let us determine, if we can, what will satisfy them.

Will they be satisfied if the Territories be unconditionally surrendered to them? We know they will not. In all their present complaints against us, the Territories are scarcely mentioned. Invasions and insurrections are the rage now. Will it satisfy them, if, in the future, we have nothing to do with invasions and insurrections? We know it will not. We so know, because we know we never had anything to do with invasions and insurrections; and yet this total abstaining does not exempt us from the charge and the denunciation.

The question recurs, what will satisfy them? Simply this: We must not only let them alone, but we must, somehow, convince them that we do let them alone. This, we know by experience, is no easy task. We have been so trying to convince them from the very beginning of our organization, but with no success. In all our platforms and speeches we have constantly protested our purpose to let them alone; but this has had no tendency to convince them. Alike unavailing to convince them, is the fact that they have never detected a man of us in any attempt to disturb them.

These natural, and apparently adequate means all failing, what will convince them? This, and this only: cease to call slavery wrong, and join them in calling it right. And this must be done thoroughly---done in acts as well as in words. Silence will not be tolerated---we must place ourselves avowedly with them. Senator Douglas's new sedition law must be enacted and enforced, suppressing all declarations that slavery is wrong, whether made in politics, in presses, in pulpits, or in private. We must arrest and return their fugitive slaves with greedy pleasure. We must pull down our Free State constitutions. The whole atmosphere must be disinfected from all taint of opposition to slavery, before they will cease to believe that all their troubles proceed from us.

I am quite aware they do not state their case precisely in this way. Most of them would probably say to us, "Let us alone, do nothing to us, and say what you please about slavery." But we do let them alone---have never disturbed them---so that, after all, it is what we say, which dissatisfies them. They will continue to accuse us of doing, until we cease saying.

I am also aware they have not, as yet, in terms, demanded the overthrow of our Free-State Constitutions. Yet those Constitutions declare the wrong of slavery, with more solemn emphasis, than do all other sayings against it; and when all these other sayings shall have been silenced, the overthrow of these Constitutions will be demanded, and nothing be left to resist the demand. It is nothing to the contrary, that they do not demand the whole of this just now. Demanding what they do, and for the reason they do, they can voluntarily stop nowhere short of this consummation. Holding, as they do, that slavery is morally right, and socially elevating, they cannot cease to demand a full national recognition of it, as a legal right, and a social blessing.

Nor can we justifiably withhold this, on any ground save our conviction that slavery is wrong. If slavery is right, all words, acts, laws, and constitutions against it, are themselves wrong, and should be silenced, and swept away. If it is right, we cannot justly object to its nationality---its universality; if it is wrong, they cannot justly insist upon its extension---its enlargement. All they ask, we could readily grant, if we thought slavery right; all we ask, they could as readily grant, if they thought it wrong. Their thinking it right, and our thinking it wrong, is the precise fact upon which depends the whole controversy. Thinking it right, as they do, they are not to blame for desiring its full recognition, as being right; but, thinking it wrong, as we do, can we yield to them? Can we cast our votes with their view, and against our own? In view of our moral, social, and political responsibilities, can we do this?

Wrong as we think slavery is, we can yet afford to let it alone where it is, because that much is due to the necessity arising from its actual presence in the nation; but can we, while our votes will prevent it, allow it to spread into the National Territories, and to overrun us here in these Free States? If our sense of duty forbids this, then let us stand by our duty, fearlessly and effectively. Let us be diverted by none of those sophistical contrivances wherewith we are so industriously plied and belabored---contrivances such as groping for some middle ground between the right and the wrong, vain as the search for a man who should be neither a living man nor a dead man---such as a policy of "don't care" on a question about which all true men do care---such as Union appeals beseeching true Union men to yield to Disunionists, reversing the divine rule, and calling, not the sinners, but the righteous to repentance---such as invocations to Washington, imploring men to unsay what Washington said, and undo what Washington did.

Neither let us be slandered from our duty by false accusations against us, nor frightened from it by menaces of destruction to the Government nor of dungeons to ourselves. LET US HAVE FAITH THAT RIGHT MAKES MIGHT, AND IN THAT FAITH, LET US, TO THE END, DARE TO DO OUR DUTY AS WE UNDERSTAND IT.

THE END OF SLAVERY

Lincoln had pledged that, if elected, he would not permit slavery to expand into the western territories. With his election, then, that component of the national debate over slavery was settled. Indeed, the "debate" now became decidedly one-sided as the majority of southern states no longer considered themselves part of the Union. For Lincoln, however, the issue of slavery was still directly related to his war-effort. That he was unclear as to the exact nature of that relationship is apparent in his message to Congress of March 1862, where Lincoln returns to the concept of compensated emancipation as a means of ending both slavery and the war. By the summer of that year, however, he determined to attack the institution of slavery as a means of undermining the Southern war effort, and thus the

Emancipation Proclamation began to take shape. In September, following the Battle of Antietam, a Union victory that Lincoln and his cabinet believed would enhance the effect of the proclamation, the preliminary Emancipation Proclamation was announced. The proclamation had little immediate impact on the condition of slaves, yet the document undeniably altered the course of the war and expanded its aims. No longer simply a war to put down a rebellion, Lincoln's war effort was now inextricably linked to the issue of slavery. The next year, using the public forum of a published letter accepting an honorary membership in the New York Workingmen's Democratic Republican Association, Lincoln returned to a theme he had used often in his presidential campaign and again in his first Message to Congress in December 1861. Slavery, he warned, was not only an affront to the working man but a very real threat to the virtues associated with free labor. In August 1864, Lincoln responded to a letter from Charles D. Robinson, a newspaper editor from Wisconsin, and attempted to bring some clarity to his views on slavery and Union. Admittedly, he wrote, his first objective was to save the Union, but at the same time he made it clear that there was no retreat from emancipation. While many details remained to be resolved, freedom, Lincoln wrote, once offered, cannot be rescinded.

Message to Congress, March 6, 1862

Fellow-citizens of the Senate, and House of Representatives,

I recommend the adoption of a Joint Resolution by your honorable bodies which shall be substantially as follows:

"Resolved that the United States ought to co-operate with any state which may adopt gradual abolishment of slavery, giving to such state pecuniary aid, to be used by such state in it's discretion, to compensate for the inconveniences public and private, produced by such change of system"

If the proposition contained in the resolution does not meet the approval of Congress and the country, there is the end; but if it does command such approval, I deem it of importance that the states and people immediately interested, should be at once distinctly notified of the fact, so that they may begin to consider whether to accept or reject it. The federal government would find it's highest interest in such a measure, as one of the most efficient means of self-preservation. The leaders of the existing insurrection entertain the hope that this government will ultimately be forced to acknowledge the independence of some part of the disaffected region, and that all the slave states North of such part will then say "the Union, for which we have struggled, being already gone, we now choose to go with the Southern section." To deprive them of this hope, substantially ends the rebellion; and the initiation of emancipation completely deprives them of it, as to all the states initiating it. The point is not that all the states tolerating slavery would very soon, if at all, initiate emancipation; but that, while the offer is equally made to all, the more Northern shall, by such initiation, make it certain to the more Southern, that in no event, will the former ever join the latter, in their proposed confederacy. I say "initiation" because, in my judgment, gradual, and not sudden emancipation, is better for all. In the mere financial, or pecuniary view, any member of Congress, with the census-tables and Treasury-reports before him, can readily see for himself how very soon the current expenditures of this war would purchase, at fair valuation, all the slaves in any named State. Such a proposition, on the part of the general government, sets up no claim of a right, by federal authority, to interfere with slavery within state limits, referring, as it does, the absolute control of the subject, in each case, to the state and it's people, immediately interested. It is proposed as a matter of perfectly free choice with them.

In the annual message last December, I thought fit to say "The Union must be preserved; and hence all indispensable means must be employed." I said this, not hastily, but deliberately. War has been made, and continues to be, an indispensable means to this end. A practical re-acknowledgement of the national authority would render the war unnecessary, and it would at once cease. If, however, resistance continues, the war must also continue; and it is impossible to foresee all the incidents, which may attend and all the ruin which may follow it. Such as may seem indispensable, or may obviously promise great efficiency towards ending the struggle, must and will come.

The proposition now made, though an offer only, I hope it may be esteemed no offence to ask whether the pecuniary consideration tendered would not be of more value to the States and private persons concerned, than are the institution, and property in it, in the present aspect of affairs.

While it is true that the adoption of the proposed resolution would be merely initiatory, and not within itself a practical measure, it is recommended in the hope that it would soon lead to important practical results. In full view of my great responsibility to my God, and to my country, I earnestly beg the attention of Congress and the people to the subject. ABRAHAM LINCOLN

March 6. 1862.

Emancipation Proclamation, January 1, 1863

By the President of the United States of America:

A Proclamation.

Whereas, on the twenty second day of September, in the year of our Lord one thousand eight hundred and sixty two, a proclamation was issued by the President of the United States, containing, among other things, the following, to wit:

That on the first day of January, in the year of our Lord one thousand eight hundred and sixty-three, all persons held as slaves within any State or designated part of a State, the people whereof shall then be in rebellion against the United States, shall be then, thenceforward, and forever free; and the Executive Government of the United States, including the military and naval authority thereof, will recognize and maintain the freedom of such persons, and will do no act or acts to repress such persons, or any of them, in any efforts they may make for their actual freedom.

"That the Executive will, on the first day of January aforesaid, by proclamation, designate the States and parts of States, if any, in which the people thereof, respectively, shall then be in rebellion against the United States; and the fact that any State, or the people thereof, shall on that day be, in good faith, represented in the Congress of the United States by members chosen thereto at elections wherein a majority of the qualified voters of such State shall have participated, shall, in the absence of strong countervailing testimony, be deemed conclusive evidence that such State, and the people thereof, are not then in rebellion against the United States."

Now, therefore I, Abraham Lincoln, President of the United States, by virtue of the power in me vested as Commander-in-Chief, of the Army and Navy of the United States in time of actual armed rebellion against authority and government of the United States, and as a fit and necessary war measure for suppressing said rebellion, do, on this first day of January, in the year of our Lord one thousand eight hundred and sixty three, and in accordance with my purpose so to do publicly proclaimed for the full period of one hundred days, from the day first above mentioned, order and designate as the States and parts of States wherein the people thereof respectively, are this day in rebellion against the United States, the following, to wit:

Arkansas, Texas, Louisiana, (except the Parishes of St. Bernard, Plaquemines, Jefferson, St. Johns, St. Charles, St. James[,] Ascension, Assumption, Terrebonne, Lafourche, St. Mary, St. Martin, and Orleans, including the City of New-Orleans) Mississippi, Alabama, Florida, Georgia, South-Carolina, North-Carolina, and Virginia, (except the forty eight counties designated as West Virginia, and also the counties of Berkley, Accomac, Northampton, Elizabeth-City, York, Princess Ann, and Norfolk, including the cities of Norfolk & Portsmouth [)]; and which excepted parts are, for the present, left precisely as if this proclamation were not issued.

And by virtue of the power, and for the purpose aforesaid, I do order and declare that all persons held as slaves within said designated States, and parts of States, are, and henceforward shall be free; and that the Executive government of the United States, including the military and naval authorities thereof, will recognize and maintain the freedom of said persons.

And I hereby enjoin upon the people so declared to be free to abstain from all violence, unless in necessary self-defence; and I recommend to them that, in all cases when allowed, they labor faithfully for reasonable wages.

And I further declare and make known, that such persons of suitable condition, will be received into the armed service of the United States to garrison forts, positions, stations, and other places, and to man vessels of all sorts in said service.

And upon this act, sincerely believed to be an act of justice, warranted by the Constitution, upon military necessity, I invoke the considerate judgment of mankind, and the gracious favor of Almighty God.

In witness whereof, I have hereunto set my hand and caused the seal of the United States to be affixed.

Done at the City of Washington, this first day of January, in the year of our Lord one thousand eight hundred and sixty three, and of the Independence of the United States of America the eighty-seventh.

[L.S.]
By the President: ABRAHAM LINCOLN
WILLIAM H. SEWARD, Secretary of State.

Reply to New York Workingmen's Democratic Republican Association, March 21, 1864

March 21, 1864

Gentlemen of the Committee.

The honorary membership in your Association, as generously tendered, is gratefully accepted.

You comprehend, as your address shows, that the existing rebellion, means more, and tends to more, than the perpetuation of African Slavery---that it is, in fact, a war upon the rights of all working people. Partly to show that this view has not escaped my attention, and partly that I cannot better express myself, I read a passage from the Message to Congress in December 1861:

It continues to develop that the insurrection is largely, if not exclusively, a war upon the first principle of popular government---the rights of the people. Conclusive evidence of this is found in the most grave and maturely considered public documents, as well as in the general tone of the insurgents. In those documents we find the abridgement of the existing right of suffrage and the denial to the people of all right to participate in the selection of public officers, except the legislative boldly advocated, with labored arguments to prove that large control of the people in government, is the source of all political evil. Monarchy itself is sometimes hinted at as a possible refuge from the power of the people.

In my present position, I could scarcely be justified were I to omit raising a warning voice against this approach of returning despotism.

It is not needed, nor fitting here, that a general argument should be made in favor of popular institutions; but there is one point, with its connexions, not so hackneyed as most others, to which I ask a brief attention. It is the effort to place capital on an equal footing with, if not above labor, in the structure of government. It is assumed that labor is available only in connexion with capital; that nobody labors unless somebody else, owning capital, somehow by the use of it, induces him to labor. This assumed, it is next considered whether it is best that capital shall hire laborers, and thus induce them to work by their own consent, or buy them, and drive them to it without their consent. Having proceeded so far, it is naturally concluded that all laborers are either hired laborers, or what we call slaves. And further it is assumed that whoever is once a hired laborer, is fixed in that condition for life.

Now, there is no such relation between capital and labor as assumed; nor is there any such thing as a free man being fixed for life in the condition of a hired laborer. Both these assumptions are false, and all inferences from them are groundless.

Labor is prior to, and independent of, capital. Capital is only the fruit of labor, and could never have existed if labor had not first existed. Labor is the superior of capital, and deserves much the higher consideration. Capital has its rights, which are as worthy of protection as any other rights. Nor is it denied that there is, and probably always will be, a relation between labor and capital, producing mutual benefits. The error is in assuming that the whole labor of community exists within that relation. A few men own capital, and that few avoid labor themselves, and, with their capital, hire or buy another few to labor for them. A large majority belong to neither class---neither work for others, nor have others working for them. In most of the southern States, a majority of the whole people of all colors are neither slaves nor masters; while in the northern a large majority are neither hirers nor hired. Men with their families---wives, sons, and daughters---work for themselves, on their farms, in their houses, and in their shops, taking the whole product to themselves, and asking no favors of capital on the one hand, nor of hired laborers or slaves on the other. It is not forgotten that a considerable number of persons mingle their own labor with capital---that is, they labor with their own hands, and also buy or hire others to labor for them; but this is only a mixed, and not a distinct class. No principle stated is disturbed by the existence of this mixed class.

Again: as has already been said, there is not, of necessity, any such thing as the free hired laborer being fixed to that condition for life. Many independent men everywhere in these States, a few years back in their lives, were hired laborers. The prudent, penniless beginner in the world, labors for wages awhile, saves a surplus with which to buy tools or land for himself; then labors on his own account another while, and at length hires another new beginner to help him. This is the just, and generous, and prosperous system, which opens the way to all---gives hope to all, and consequent energy, and progress, and improvement of condition to all. No men living are more worthy to be trusted than those who toil up from poverty---none less inclined to take, or touch, aught which they have not honestly earned. Let them beware of surrendering a political power which they already possess, and which, if surrendered, will surely be used to close the door of advancement against such as they, and to fix new disabilities and burdens upon them, till all of liberty shall be lost.

The views then expressed remain unchanged, nor have I much to add. None are so deeply interested to resist the present rebellion as the working people. Let them beware of prejudice, working division and hostility among themselves. The most notable feature of a disturbance in your city last summer, was the hanging of some working people by other working people. It should never be so. The strongest bond of human sympathy, outside of the family relation, should be one uniting all working people, of all nations, and tongues, and kindreds. Nor should this lead to a war upon property, or the owners of property. Property is the fruit of labor ---property is desirable --- --- is a positive good in the world. That some should be rich, shows that others may become rich, and hence is just encouragement to industry and enterprize. Let not him who is houseless pull down the house of another; but let him labor diligently and build one for himself, thus by example assuring that his own shall be safe from violence when built.

To Charles D. Robinson, August 17, 1864

Hon. Charles D. Robinson

Washington, Executive Mansion, August 17, 1864.

My dear Sir:

Your letter of the 7th was placed in my hand yesterday by Gov. Randall.

To me it seems plain that saying re-union and abandonment of slavery would be considered, if offered, is not saying that nothing else or less would be considered, if offered. But I will not stand upon the mere construction of language. It is true, as you remind me, that in the Greeley letter of 1862, I said: "If I could save the Union without freeing any slaves I would do it; and if I could save it by freeing all the slaves I would do it; and if I could save it by freeing some, and leaving others alone I would also do that." I continued in the same letter as follows: "What I do about slavery and the colored race, I do because I believe it helps to save the Union; and what I forbear I forbear because I do not believe it would help to save the Union. I shall do less whenever I shall believe what I am doing hurts the cause; and I shall do more whenever I shall believe doing more will help the cause." All this I said in the utmost sincerety; and I am as true to the whole of it now, as when I first said it. When I afterwards proclaimed emancipation, and employed colored soldiers, I only followed the declaration just quoted from the Greeley letter that "I shall do more whenever I shall believe doing more will help the cause" The way these measures were to help the cause, was not to be by magic, or miracles, but by inducing the colored people to come bodily over from the rebel side to ours. On this point, nearly a year ago, in a letter to Mr. Conkling, made public at once, I wrote as follows: "But negroes, like other people, act upon motives. Why should they do anything for us if we will do nothing for them? If they stake their lives for us they must be prompted by the strongest motive---even the promise of freedom. And the promise, being made, must be kept." I am sure you will not, on due reflection, say that the promise being made, must be broken at the first opportunity. I am sure you would not desire me to say, or to leave an inference, that I am ready, whenever convenient, to join in re-enslaving those who shall have served us in consideration of our promise. As matter of morals, could such treachery by any possibility, escape the curses of Heaven, or of any good man? As matter of policy, to announce such a purpose, would ruin the Union cause itself. All recruiting of colored men would instantly cease, and all colored men now in our service, would instantly desert us. And rightfully too. Why should they give their lives for us, with full notice of our purpose to betray them? Drive back to the support of the rebellion the physical force which the colored people now give, and promise us, and neither the present, nor any coming administration, can save the Union. Take from us, and give to the enemy, the hundred and thirty, forty, or fifty thousand colored persons now serving us as soldiers, seamen, and laborers, and we can not longer maintain the contest. The party who could elect a President on a War & Slavery Restoration platform, would, of necessity, lose the colored force; and that force being lost, would be as powerless to save the Union as to do any other impossible thing. It is not a question of sentiment or taste, but one of physical force, which may be measured, and estimated as horsepower, and steam power, are measured and estimated. And by measurement, it is more than we can lose, and live. Nor can we, by discarding it, get a white force in place of it. There is a witness in every white mans bosom that he would rather go to the war having the negro to help him, than to help the enemy against him. It is not the giving of one class for another. It is simply giving a large force to the enemy, for nothing in return.

In addition to what I have said, allow me to remind you that no one, having control of the rebel armies, or, in fact, having any influence whatever in the rebellion, has offered, or intimated a willingness to, a restoration of the Union, in any event, or on any condition whatever. Let it be constantly borne in mind that no such offer has been made or intimated. Shall we be weak enough to allow the enemy to distract us with an abstract question which he himself refuses to present as a practical one? In the Conkling letter before mentioned, I said: "Whenever you shall have conquered all resistance to the Union, if I shall urge you to continue fighting, it will be an apt time then to declare that you will not fight to free negroes." I repeat this now. If Jefferson Davis wishes, for himself, or for the benefit of his friends at the North, to know what I would do if he were to offer peace and re-union, saying nothing about slavery, let him try me.

From *Collected Works*. Abraham Lincoln Association, Springfield, IL. Roy P. Basler, editor; Marion Dolores Pratt and Lloyd A. Dunlap, assistant editors. Lincoln, Abraham, 1809-1865. New Brunswick, N.J.: Rutgers University Press, 1953. Copyright © The Abraham Lincoln Association. Reprinted by permission.

Part Three

Lincoln and the Presidency

On February 11, 1861, Lincoln and his family boarded a special train for the trip to Washington D.C. for his inauguration. Rather than traveling directly to the capital, the train took a circuitous route and made numerous stops along the way to allow Lincoln to introduce himself to the people who had elected him president. The route took Lincoln through Indiana, Ohio, and on to Pittsburgh and Cleveland, then turned northeast to Buffalo, across New York to Albany, before finally heading south to New York City and across New Jersey to Philadelphia. From there, Lincoln continued on a special train, traveling incognito through Baltimore in order to foil an alleged assassination plot, before arriving in Washington on February 23. For most of the people along the way, it was their first opportunity to see and hear their new president—the first born west of the Appalachian Mountains—and they easily identified with his "Railsplitter" image. Lincoln repeatedly acknowledged, as he did in his farewell address at Springfield, the magnitude of the task of preserving the Union. Lincoln delivered his message with conviction and passion; there was no mistaking his devotion to the Union and to the principles of the founders as espoused in the Declaration of Independence. Lincoln wanted and needed to rally the country, but he also hoped to unify the various political constituencies within his own party and gain the support of those Americans who did not vote for him in order to form an effective political coalition that would enable him to govern the country and address the crisis of secession.

It was a crisis that was broadening even as Lincoln boarded the train to begin his trip to Washington. Representatives from seven southern states were in the midst of a convention in Montgomery, Alabama. They had already formed an independent government and adopted a provisional Constitution, and before Lincoln's trip was over, Jefferson Davis was sworn in as their provisional president. This new government, calling itself the Confederate

States of America, promptly authorized the seceded state governments to use their local militia to seize all United States property within their borders, a process that many of those states had already started.

The crisis escalated within hours of Lincoln's inauguration on March 4, 1861. That night when he returned to the White House, he was greeted by acting Secretary of War Joshua Holt. Holt presented him with the dispatches from Fort Sumter, a Federal stronghold in Charleston Harbor. Lincoln was aware that Confederate authorities had demanded the surrender of the fort; now he learned that the fort's commander, Major Robert Anderson, believed that Sumter was indefensible and that major reinforcements would be necessary in order to prevent surrender. Lincoln called on his cabinet for advice but their debate showed a wide divergence of opinions as to what ought to be done: some advocated immediate surrender while others called for sending reinforcements to defend the fort. Lincoln's decision found the middle road between these options; he decided to resupply rather than reinforce the fort, hoping that food and medical supplies, as opposed to troops and ammunition, would maintain the status quo and avoid a confrontation. Instead, Confederate President Jefferson Davis demanded the immediate surrender of Fort Sumter and when Anderson refused, Confederate batteries opened fire at 4:30 in the morning of April 12. After 30 hours of bombardment, Anderson agreed to a truce and surrendered the fort later that day.

Lincoln might have taken some comfort in the fact that he had managed the situation in such a way that it was the Confederates who had fired the first shot. He had kept the promise made at his inauguration to protect federal property yet not to initiate an attack against the seceded southern states. But the crisis was now escalated to open war, far beyond what anyone could have expected. It worsened when Lincoln called for 75,000 volunteers to put down the rebellion, which caused four additional states to secede and join the Confederacy. Even so, Lincoln had signaled his intention to preserve the Union by any means necessary, including some measures that went well beyond military might, including suspension of *Habeas corpus*. Lincoln was within his rights as president to take such a drastic step, but his actions nonetheless represented to many people an unnecessary and alarming expansion of presidential power. Indeed, there were many in the nation who saw such a move as further evidence that Lincoln's abilities and skills were inadequate to the monumental task that confronted the nation. Many of Lincoln's own generals worried about his lack of military background at a time when the fate of the nation was to be decided by war. Few took Lincoln seriously as commander-in-chief, and some openly berated him. Lincoln, himself, understood that he was not qualified to formulate and execute strategy, but he did understand the tremendous advantages that the North had in terms of resources and manpower. And, as he had done throughout his life when he needed to understand an issue, he educated himself and before the war was over, he had become a very effective commander-in-chief.

As the battles intensified, Lincoln found himself increasingly obliged to explain the terrible costs of war. It was not uncommon for him to take time to respond personally to those who were widowed and orphaned by the conflict. The personal losses he himself had endured in his earlier years meant that he was familiar with death, and could explain to the nation why the sacrifices that were imposed on them were necessary. Equally important, Lincoln was able to let others see that he understood the pain and loss they were forced to endure.

But he also recognized that his greatest challenge might well come after the war was over. Aside from the enormous social and political challenges of transitioning four-and-a-half million former slaves to freedom—and, in the process, laying the groundwork for social and political equality—Lincoln knew that the status of the seceded states was certain to be a controversial issue. For him, the solution was easy enough; once the Southern states had written and adopted new constitutions that abolished slavery, they would be readmitted into the Union. There were other details, to be sure, but his vision was not complicated; the nation should move quickly beyond the bitterness and anger created by the war, and become a unified nation as soon as possible.

TAKING CHARGE

Lincoln's efforts to take charge of the crisis confronting the nation began even before he arrived in Washington. The first selection here, Lincoln's speech at Philadelphia on February 22, 1861, was the last of many such speeches he delivered en route to his inauguration. It clearly illustrates his view of the secession crisis and acknowledges his responsibility as president and commander-in-chief to find a resolution. But Lincoln also expresses a reluctance to use force and suggests that the responsibility of war with all its consequences lies with the secessionists.

Ten days later Lincoln was inaugurated as president and gave the speech that the entire nation—both north and south—was most anxious to hear. His pledge to protect federal property, while at the same time promising not to attack the South, seemed to create a situation that would require him to renege on one or the other of his commitments. The force of his address, however, came with an appeal to the nation to draw upon its common history and to the South in particular to renounce secession.

The immediate crisis, of course, was in Charleston harbor where a small garrison of Federal troops was under siege. As Lincoln searched for a solution he came under attack, as he often did throughout the war, for a failure of leadership. Yet this attack came from within his cabinet. Secretary of State William Seward, once Lincoln's chief rival within the Republican Party and widely considered to be better qualified for president than Lincoln, had taken Lincoln to task for failing to formulate and implement a policy to resolve the crisis in Fort Sumter and hinted that Lincoln ought to delegate that responsibility to "some member of his cabinet." Lincoln responded immediately, although it is not clear whether the response was actually delivered or if Lincoln might have decided to meet with Seward in person. In any case, Lincoln's difficulties in organizing and managing his cabinet during the early stages of his administration and in the midst of a crisis, is clear. Equally obvious in Lincoln's response is his determination to be the president and commander-in-chief, not just in name but in fact—to make his own decisions and then take responsibility for the consequences of those decisions.

Perhaps none of those decisions in the first few months of the war had greater consequences than Lincoln's decision to suspend *Habeas corpus*. He justified the suspension of the cherished right as a necessary measure for suppressing the insurrection, then broadly defined insurrection to include "all rebels and insurgents, their aiders and abettors within the United States." This sweeping proclamation included here followed a limited and more specific suspension issued earlier.

Such a broad use of executive power, unsurprisingly, drew much criticism. Yet Lincoln understood the unique nature of a civil war, and the very real threat posed by domestic enemies of the government. At the same time, he understood that there were international considerations that must be taken into account. His letter to the Workingmen of Manchester, England, demonstrates that he grasped the importance of a clear and effective explanation of his war aims to a European audience.

Speech in Independence Hall, Philadelphia, Pennsylvania, February 22, 1861

Mr. CUYLER:---I am filled with deep emotion at finding myself standing here in the place where were collected together the wisdom, the patriotism, the devotion to principle, from which sprang the institutions under which we live. You have kindly suggested to me that in my hands is the task of restoring peace to our distracted country. I can say in return, sir, that all the political sentiments I entertain have been drawn, so far as I have been able to draw them, from the sentiments which originated, and were given to the world from this hall in which we stand. I have never had a feeling politically that did not spring from the sentiments embodied in the Declaration of Independence. (Great cheering.) I have often pondered over the dangers which were incurred by the men who assembled here and adopted that Declaration of Independence---I have pondered over the toils that were endured by the officers and soldiers of the army, who achieved that Independence. (Applause.) I have often inquired of myself, what great principle or idea it was that kept this Confederacy so long together. It was not the mere matter of the separation of the colonies from the mother land; but something in that Declaration giving liberty, not alone to the people of this country, but hope to the world for all future time. (Great applause.) It was that which gave promise that in due time the weights should be lifted from the shoulders of all men, and that all should have an equal chance. (Cheers.) This is the sentiment embodied in that Declaration of Independence.

Now, my friends, can this country be saved upon that basis? If it can, I will consider myself one of the happiest men in the world if I can help to save it. If it can't be saved upon that principle, it will be truly awful. But, if this country cannot be saved without giving up that principle---I was about to say I would rather be assassinated on this spot than to surrender it. (Applause.)

Now, in my view of the present aspect of affairs, there is no need of bloodshed and war. There is no necessity for it. I am not in favor of such a course, and I may say in advance, there will be no blood shed unless it be forced upon the Government. The Government will not use force unless force is used against it. (Prolonged applause and cries of "That's the proper sentiment.")

My friends, this is a wholly unprepared speech. I did not expect to be called upon to say a word when I came here---I supposed I was merely to do something towards raising a flag. I may, therefore, have said something indiscreet, (cries of "no, no"), but I have said nothing but what I am willing to live by, and, in the pleasure of Almighty God, die by.

First Inaugural Address, March 4, 1861

Fellow citizens of the United States:

In compliance with a custom as old as the government itself, I appear before you to address you briefly, and to take, in your presence, the oath prescribed by the Constitution of the United States, to be taken by the President "before he enters on the execution of his office."

I do not consider it necessary, at present, for me to discuss those matters of administration about which there is no special anxiety, or excitement.

Apprehension seems to exist among the people of the Southern States, that by the accession of a Republican Administration, their property, and their peace, and personal security, are to be endangered. There has never been any reasonable cause for such apprehension. Indeed, the most ample evidence to the contrary has all the while existed, and been open to their inspection. It is found in nearly all the published speeches of him who now addresses you.

I do but quote from one of those speeches when I declare that "I have no purpose, directly or indirectly, to interfere with the institution of slavery in the States where it exists. I believe I have no lawful right to do so, and I have no inclination to do so." Those who nominated and elected me did so with full knowledge that I had made this, and many similar declarations, and had never recanted them. And more than this, they placed in the platform, for my acceptance, and as a law to themselves, and to me, the clear and emphatic resolution which I now read:

"Resolved, That the maintenance inviolate of the rights of the States, and especially the right of each State to order and control its own domestic institutions according to its own judgment exclusively, is essential to that balance of power on which the perfection and endurance of our political fabric depend; and we denounce the lawless invasion by armed force of the soil of any State or Territory, no matter under what pretext, as among the gravest of crimes."

I now reiterate these sentiments: and in doing so, I only press upon the public attention the most conclusive evidence of which the case is susceptible, that the property, peace and security of no section are to be in anywise endangered by the now incoming Administration. I add too, that all the protection which, consistently with the Constitution and the laws, can be given, will be cheerfully given to all the States when lawfully demanded, for whatever cause---as cheerfully to one section, as to another.

There is much controversy about the delivering up of fugitives from service or labor. The clause I now read is as plainly written in the Constitution as any other of its provisions:

"No person held to service or labor in one State, under the laws thereof, escaping into another, shall, in consequence of any law or regulation therein, be discharged from such service or labor, but shall be delivered up on claim of the party to whom such service or labor may be due."

It is scarcely questioned that this provision was intended by those who made it, for the reclaiming of what we call fugitive slaves; and the intention of the law-giver is the law. All members of Congress swear their support to the whole Constitution---to this provision as much as to any other. To the proposition, then, that slaves whose cases come within the terms of this clause, "shall be delivered up," their oaths are unanimous. Now, if they would make the effort in good temper, could they not, with nearly equal unanimity, frame and pass a law, by means of which to keep good that unanimous oath?

There is some difference of opinion whether this clause should be enforced by national or by state authority; but surely that difference is not a very material one. If the slave is to be surrendered, it can be of but little consequence to him, or to others, by which authority it is done. And should any one, in any case, be content that his oath shall go unkept, on a merely unsubstantial controversy as to how it shall be kept?

Again, in any law upon this subject, ought not all the safeguards of liberty known in civilized and humane jurisprudence to be introduced, so that a free man be not, in any case, surrendered as a slave? And might it not be well, at the same time, to provide by law for the enforcement of that clause in the Constitution which guarranties that "The citizens of each State shall be entitled to all previleges and immunities of citizens in the several States?"

I take the official oath to-day, with no mental reservations, and with no purpose to construe the Constitution or laws, by any hypercritical rules. And while I do not choose now to specify particular acts of Congress as proper to be enforced, I do suggest, that it will be much safer for all, both in official and private stations, to conform to, and abide by, all those acts which stand unrepealed, than to violate any of them, trusting to find impunity in having them held to be unconstitutional.

It is seventy-two years since the first inauguration of a President under our national Constitution. During that period fifteen different and greatly distinguished citizens, have, in succession, administered the executive branch of the government. They have conducted it through many perils; and, generally, with great success. Yet, with all this scope for precedent, I now enter upon the same task for the brief constitutional term of four years, under great and peculiar difficulty. A disruption of the Federal Union heretofore only menaced, is now formidably attempted.

I hold, that in contemplation of universal law, and of the Constitution, the Union of these States is perpetual. Perpetuity is implied, if not expressed, in the fundamental law of all national governments. It is safe to assert that no government proper, ever had a provision in its organic law for its own termination. Continue to execute all the express provisions of our national Constitution, and the Union will endure forever---it being impossible to destroy it, except by some action not provided for in the instrument itself.

Again, if the United States be not a government proper, but an association of States in the nature of contract merely, can it, as a contract, be peaceably unmade, by less than all the parties who made it? One party to a contract may violate it--- break it, so to speak; but does it not require all to lawfully rescind it?

Descending from these general principles, we find the proposition that, in legal contemplation, the Union is perpetual, confirmed by the history of the Union itself. The Union is much older than the Constitution. It was formed in fact, by the Articles of Association in 1774. It was matured and continued by the Declaration of Independence in 1776. It was further matured and the faith of all the then thirteen States expressly plighted and engaged that it should be perpetual, by the Articles of Confederation in 1778. And finally, in 1787, one of the declared objects for ordaining and establishing the Constitution, was "to form a more perfect union."

But if destruction of the Union, by one, or by a part only, of the States, be lawfully possible, the Union is less perfect than before the Constitution, having lost the vital element of perpetuity.

It follows from these views that no State, upon its own mere motion, can lawfully get out of the Union,---that resolves and ordinances to that effect are legally void; and that acts of violence, within any State or States, against the authority of the United States, are insurrectionary or revolutionary, according to circumstances.

I therefore consider that, in view of the Constitution and the laws, the Union is unbroken; and, to the extent of my ability, I shall take care, as the Constitution itself expressly enjoins upon me, that the laws of the Union be faithfully executed in all the States. Doing this I deem to be only a simple duty on my part; and I shall perform it, so far as practicable, unless my rightful masters, the American people, shall withhold the requisite means, or, in some authoritative manner, direct the contrary. I trust this ill not be regarded as a menace, but only as the declared purpose of the Union that it will constitutionally defend, and maintain itself.

In doing this there needs to be no bloodshed or violence; and there shall be none, unless it be forced upon the national authority. The power the confided to me, will be used to hold, occupy, and possess the property, and places belonging to the government, and to collect the duties and imposts; but beyond what may be necessary for these objects, there will be no invasion---no using of force against, or among the people anywhere. Where hostility to the United States, in any interior locality, shall be so great and so universal, as to prevent competent resident citizens from holding the Federal offices, there will be no attempt to force obnoxious strangers among the people for that object. While the strict legal right may exist in the government to enforce the exercise of these offices, the attempt to do so would be so irritating, and so nearly impracticable with all, that I deem it better to forego, for the time, the uses of such offices.

The mails, unless repelled, will continue to be furnished in all parts of the Union. So far as possible, the people everywhere shall have that sense of perfect security which is most favorable to calm thought and reflection. The course here indicated will be followed, unless current events, and experience, shall show a modification, or change, to be proper; and in every case and exigency, my best discretion will be exercised, according to circumstances actually existing, and with a view and a hope of a peaceful solution of the national troubles, and the restoration of fraternal sympathies and affections.

That there are persons in one section, or another who seek to destroy the Union at all events, and are glad of any pretext to do it, I will neither affirm or deny; but if there be such, I need address no word to them. To those, however, who really love the Union, may I not speak?

Before entering upon so grave a matter as the destruction of our national fabric, with all its benefits, its memories, and its hopes, would it not be wise to ascertain precisely why we do it? Will you hazard so desperate a step, while there is any possibility that any portion of the ills you fly from, have no real existence? Will you, while the certain ills you fly to, are greater than all the real ones you fly from? Will you risk the commission of so fearful a mistake?

All profess to be content in the Union, if all constitutional rights can be maintained. Is it true, then, that any right, plainly written in the Constitution, has been denied? I think not. Happily the human mind is so constituted, that no party can reach to the audacity of doing this. Think, if you can, of a single instance in which a plainly written provision of the Constitution has ever been denied. If, by the mere force of numbers, a majority should deprive a minority of any clearly written constitutional right, it might, in a moral point of view, justify revolution---certainly would, if such right were a vital one. But such is not our case. All the vital rights of minorities, and of individuals, are so plainly assured to them, by affirmations and negations, guarranties and prohibitions, in the Constitution, that controversies never arise concerning them. But no organic law can ever be framed with a provision specifically applicable to every question which may occur in practical administration. No foresight can anticipate, nor any document of reasonable length contain express provisions for all possible questions. Shall fugitives from labor be surrendered by national or by State authority? The Constitution does not expressly say. May Congress prohibit slavery in the territories? The Constitution does not expressly say. Must Congress protect slavery in the territories? The Constitution does not expressly say.

From questions of this class spring all our constitutional controversies, and we divide upon them into majorities and minorities. If the minority will not acquiesce, the majority must, or the government must cease. There is no other alternative; for continuing the government, is acquiescence on one side or the other. If a minority, in such case, will secede rather than acquiesce, they make a precedent which, in turn, will divide and ruin them; for a minority of their own will secede from them, whenever a majority refuses to be controlled by such minority. For instance, why may not any portion of a new confederacy, a year or two hence, arbitrarily secede again, precisely as portions of the present Union now claim to secede from it. All who cherish disunion sentiments, are now being educated to the exact temper of doing this. Is there such perfect identity of interests among the States to compose a new Union, as to produce harmony only, and prevent renewed secession?

Plainly, the central idea of secession, is the essence of anarchy. A majority, held in restraint by constitutional checks, and limitations, and always changing easily, with deliberate changes of popular opinions and sentiments, is the only true sovereign of a free people. Whoever rejects it, does, of necessity, fly to anarchy or to despotism. Unanimity is impossible; the rule of a minority, as a permanent arrangement, is wholly inadmissable; so that, rejecting the majority principle, anarchy, or despotism in some form, is all that is left.

I do not forget the position assumed by some, that constitutional questions are to be decided by the Supreme Court; nor do I deny that such decisions must be binding in any case, upon the parties to a suit, as to the object of that suit, while they are also entitled to very high respect and consideration, in all paralel cases, by all other departments of the government. And while it is obviously possible that such decision may be erroneous in any given case, still the evil effect following it, being limited to that particular case, with the chance that it may be over-ruled, and never become a precedent for other cases, can better be borne than could the evils of a different practice. At the same time the candid citizen must confess that if the policy of the government, upon vital questions, affecting the whole people, is to be irrevocably fixed by decisions of the Supreme Court, the instant they are made, in ordinary litigation between parties, in personal actions, the people will have ceased, to be their own rulers, having, to that extent, practically resigned their government, into the hands of that eminent tribunal. Nor is there, in this view, any assault upon the court, or the judges. It is a duty, from which they may not shrink, to decide cases properly brought before them; and it is no fault of theirs, if others seek to turn their decisions to political purposes.

One section of our country believes slavery is right, and ought to be extended, while the other believes it is wrong, and ought not to be extended. This is the only substantial dispute. The fugitive slave clause of the Constitution, and the law for the suppression of the foreign slave trade, are each as well enforced, perhaps, as any law can ever be in a community where the moral sense of the people imperfectly supports the law itself. The great body of the people abide by the dry legal obligation in both cases, and a few break over in each. This, I think, cannot be perfectly cured; and it would be worse in both cases after the separation of the sections, than before. The foreign slave trade, now imperfectly suppressed, would be ultimately revived without restriction, in one section; while fugitive slaves, now only partially surrendered, would not be surrendered at all, by the other.

Physically speaking, we cannot separate. We cannot remove our respective sections from each other, nor build an impassable wall between them. A husband

and wife may be divorced, and go out of the presence, and beyond the reach of each other; but the different parts of our country cannot do this. They cannot but remain face to face; and intercourse, either amicable or hostile, must continue between them. Is it possible then to make that intercourse more advantageous, or more satisfactory, after separation than before? Can aliens make treaties easier than friends can make laws? Can treaties be more faithfully enforced between aliens, than laws can among friends? Suppose you go to war, you cannot fight always; and when, after much loss on both sides, and no gain on either, you cease fighting, the identical old questions, as to terms of intercourse, are again upon you.

This country, with its institutions, belongs to the people who inhabit it. Whenever they shall grow weary of the existing government, they can exercise their constitutional right of amending it, or their revolutionary right to dismember, or overthrow it. I can not be ignorant of the fact that many worthy, and patriotic citizens are desirous of having the national constitution amended. While I make no recommendation of amendments, I fully recognize the rightful authority of the people over the whole subject, to be exercised in either of the modes prescribed in the instrument itself; and I should, under existing circumstances, favor, rather than oppose, a fair oppertunity being afforded the people to act upon it.

I will venture to add that, to me, the convention mode seems preferable, in that it allows amendments to originate with the people themselves, instead of only permitting them to take, or reject, propositions, originated by others, not especially chosen for the purpose, and which might not be precisely such, as they would wish to either accept or refuse. I understand a proposed amendment to the Constitution---which amendment, however, I have not seen, has passed Congress, to the effect that the federal government, shall never interfere with the domestic institutions of the States, including that of persons held to service. To avoid misconstruction of what I have said, I depart from my purpose not to speak of particular amendments, so far as to say that, holding such a provision to now be implied constitutional law, I have no objection to its being made express, and irrevocable.

The Chief Magistrate derives all his authority from the people, and they have conferred none upon him to fix terms for the separation of the States. The people themselves can do this also if they choose; but the executive, as such, has nothing to do with it. His duty is to administer the present government, as it came to his hands, and to transmit it, unimpaired by him, to his successor.

Why should there not be a patient confidence in the ultimate justice of the people? Is there any better, or equal hope, in the world? In our present differences, is either party without faith of being in the right? If the Almighty Ruler of nations, with his eternal truth and justice, be on your side of the North, or on yours of the South, that truth, and that justice, will surely prevail, by the judgment of this great tribunal, the American people.

By the frame of the government under which we live, this same people have wisely given their public servants but little power for mischief; and have, with equal wisdom, provided for the return of that little to their own hands at very short intervals.

While the people retain their virtue, and vigilence, no administration, by any extreme of wickedness or folly, can very seriously injure the government, in the short space of four years.

My countrymen, one and all, think calmly and well, upon this whole subject. Nothing valuable can be lost by taking time. If there be an object to hurry any of you, in hot haste, to a step which you would never take deliberately, that object will be frustrated by taking time; but no good object can be frustrated by it. Such of you as are now dissatisfied, still have the old Constitution unimpaired, and, on the sensitive point, the laws of your own framing under it; while the new administration will have no immediate power, if it would, to change either. If it were admitted that you who are dissatisfied, hold the right side in the dispute, there still is no single good reason for precipitate action. Intelligence, patriotism, Christianity, and a firm reliance on Him, who has never yet forsaken this favored land, are still competent to adjust, in the best way, all our present difficulty.

In your hands, my dissatisfied fellow countrymen, and not in mine, is the momentous issue of civil war. The government will not assail you. You can have no conflict, without being yourselves the aggressors. You have no oath registered in Heaven to destroy the government, while I shall have the most solemn one to "preserve, protect and defend" it.

I am loth to close. We are not enemies, but friends. We must not be enemies. Though passion may have strained, it must not break our bonds of affection. The mystic chords of memory, streching from every battle-field, and patriot grave, to every living heart and hearthstone, all over this broad land, will yet swell the chorus of the Union, when again touched, as surely they will be, by the better angels of our nature.

To William H. Seward, April 1, 1861

Executive Mansion April 1, 1861

Hon: W. H. Seward:

My dear Sir: Since parting with you I have been considering your paper dated this day, and entitled "Some thoughts for the President's consideration." The first proposition in it is, "1st. We are at the end of a month's administration, and yet without a policy, either domestic or foreign."

At the beginning of that month, in the inaugeral, I said "The power confided to me will be used to hold, occupy and possess the property and places belonging to the government, and to collect the duties, and imposts." This had your distinct approval at the time; and, taken in connection with the order I immediately gave General Scott, directing him to employ every means in his power to strengthen and hold the forts, comprises the exact domestic policy you now urge, with the single exception, that it does not propose to abandon Fort Sumpter.

Again, I do not perceive how the re-inforcement of Fort Sumpter would be done on a slavery, or party issue, while that of Fort Pickens would be on a more national, and patriotic one.

The news received yesterday in regard to St. Domingo, certainly brings a new item within the range of our foreign policy; but up to that time we have been preparing circulars, and instructions to ministers, and the like, all in perfect harmony, without even a suggestion that we had no foreign policy.

Upon your closing propositions, that "whatever policy we adopt, there must be an energetic prossecution of it"

"For this purpose it must be somebody's business to pursue and direct it incessantly"

"Either the President must do it himself, and be all the while active in it, or"

"Devolve it on some member of his cabinet"
"Once adopted, debates on it must end, and all agree and abide" I remark that

if this must be done, I must do it. When a general line of policy is adopted, I apprehend there is no danger of its being changed without good reason, or continuing to be a subject of unnecessary debate; still, upon points arising in its progress, I wish, and suppose I am entitled to have the advice of all the cabinet. Your Obt. Servt. A. LINCOLN

Proclamation Suspending the Writ of *Habeas Corpus*, September 24 1862

By the President of the United States of America:

A Proclamation.

Whereas, it has become necessary to call into service not only volunteers but also portions of the militia of the States by draft in order to suppress the insurrection existing in the United States, and disloyal persons are not adequately restrained by the ordinary processes of law from hindering this measure and from giving aid and comfort in various ways to the insurrection;

Now, therefore, be it ordered, first, that during the existing insurrection and as a necessary measure for suppressing the same, all Rebels and Insurgents, their aiders and abettors within the United States, and all persons discouraging volunteer enlistments, resisting militia drafts, or guilty of any disloyal practice, affording aid and comfort to Rebels against the authority of the United States, shall be subject to martial law and liable to trial and punishment by Courts Martial or Military Commission:

Second. That the Writ of *Habeas Corpus* is suspended in respect to all persons arrested, or who are now, or hereafter during the rebellion shall be, imprisoned in any fort, camp, arsenal, military prison, or other place of confinement by any military authority or by the sentence of any Court Martial or Military Commission.

In witness whereof, I have hereunto set my hand, and caused the seal of the United States to be affixed.

[L.S.]

Done at the City of Washington this twenty fourth day of September, in the year of our Lord one thousand eight hundred and sixty-two, and of the Independence of the United States the 87th.

By the President: ABRAHAM LINCOLN.

WILLIAM H. SEWARD, Secretary of State.

To the Workingmen of Manchester, England, January 19, 1863

Executive Mansion, Washington,
January 19, 1863.

To the workingmen of Manchester:

I have the honor to acknowledge the receipt of the address and resolutions which you sent to me on the eve of the new year.

When I came, on the fourth day of March, 1861, through a free and constitutional election, to preside in the government of the United States, the country was found at the verge of civil war. Whatever might have been the cause, or whosoever the fault, one duty paramount to all others was before me, namely, to maintain and preserve at once the Constitution and the integrity of the federal republic. A conscientious purpose to perform this duty is a key to all the measures of administration which have been, and to all which will hereafter be pursued. Under our form of government, and my official oath, I could not depart from this purpose if I would. It is not always in the power of governments to enlarge or restrict the scope of moral results which follow the policies that they may deem it necessary for the public safety, from time to time, to adopt.

I have understood well that the duty of self-preservation rests solely with the American people. But I have at the same time been aware that favor or disfavor of foreign nations might have a material influence in enlarging and prolonging the struggle with disloyal men in which the country is engaged. A fair examination of history has seemed to authorize a belief that the past action and influences of the United States were generally regarded as having been beneficient towards mankind. I have therefore reckoned upon the forbearance of nations. Circumstances, to some of which you kindly allude, induced me especially to expect that if justice and good faith should be practiced by the United States, they would encounter no hostile influence on the part of Great Britain. It is now a pleasant duty to acknowledge the demonstration you have given of your desire that a spirit of peace and amity towards this country may prevail in the councils of your Queen, who is respected and esteemed in your own country only more than she is by the kindred nation which has its home on this side of the Atlantic.

I know and deeply deplore the sufferings which the workingmen at Manchester and in all Europe are called to endure in this crisis. It has been often and studiously represented that the attempt to overthrow this government, which was built upon the foundation of human rights, and to substitute for it one which should rest exclusively on the basis of human slavery, was likely to obtain the favor of Europe. Through the actions of our disloyal citizens the workingmen of Europe have been subjected to a severe trial, for the purpose of forcing their sanction to that attempt. Under these circumstances, I cannot but regard your decisive utterance upon the question as an instance of sublime Christian heroism which has not been surpassed in any age or in any country. It is, indeed, an energetic and reinspiring assurance of the inherent power of truth and of the ultimate and universal triumph of justice, humanity, and freedom. I do not doubt that the sentiments you have expressed will be sustained by your great nation, and, on the other hand, I have no hesitation in assuring you that they will excite admiration, esteem, and the most reciprocal feelings of friendship among the American people. I hail this interchange of sentiment, therefore, as an augury that, whatever else may happen, whatever misfortune may befall your country or my own, the peace and friendship which now exist between the two nations will be, as it shall be my desire to make them, perpetual.

ABRAHAM LINCOLN.

COMMANDER-IN-CHIEF

Lincoln faced enormous responsibilities as commander-in-chief. If the military effort should fail, the seceded Southern states would gain independence and the Union would fall. The selections included here reflect some of the difficulties with which he had to contend. The first document illustrates Lincoln's problems with generals whose appointments were due to political connections. John McClernand, a well-known politician from Illinois, counted himself among Lincoln's friends. McClernand was also a Democrat and Lincoln wanted very much to bring these Democrats into the Republican fold, or at least to gain their support for the war effort. Consequently, McClernand had received a commission, but his abilities as an officer were limited. Lincoln may or may not have recognized McClernand's limitations as a general, but he did recognize his value as a political ally, and so his response here seeks to soothe a bruised ego. George B. McClellan presented Lincoln with an altogether different problem. After receiving command of the Army of the Potomac, McClellan had transformed the raw recruits into a respectable fighting force. Yet his reluctance to put the army into battle constantly frustrated Lincoln. When McClellan at last set the army in motion in April 1862, his Peninsula Campaign came within six miles of the Confederate capital of Richmond. But a sudden counterattack by the Confederate army seemed to confirm his fears that he was outnumbered and outgunned. McClellan promptly ordered a retreat and then sent a letter to Secretary of War Stanton that blamed the administration for failing to support the army. Lincoln's two brief letters to McClellan included here reflect his frustration with his commanding general. In a longer letter to Secretary of State William Seward, Lincoln shows his increasingly sophisticated grasp of the military situation. By the time Joseph Hooker took command of the army in January 1863, Lincoln was obviously desperate for a victory. Although Hooker probably never intended to imply that he was willing to set himself up as a dictator, Lincoln may have believed that he did and indicated that the risk of a dictator is acceptable since such a person must first win a battle. Yet four months later at Chancellorsville, Hooker too was defeated, prompting Confederate General Robert E. Lee to launch an invasion of the North. Lincoln's frantic letters to Hooker again reveal how much he has learned about strategy, and demonstrate his decisive actions as commander-in-chief. Lincoln's search for a general with whom he could work comfortably came to an end when he brought Ulysses S. Grant east and gave him command of all Union armies. His confidence in his new commanding general is indicated in the last letter included here.

JOSEPH HOOKER, LOC

Major General Joseph Hooker. Library of Congress Prints and Photographs Division [LC-USZ62-111519].

To John A. McClernand, November 10, 1861

Washington. Nov. 10. 1861

Brigadier General McClernand

My Dear Sir This is not an official but a social letter. You have had a battle, and without being able to judge as to the precise measure of its value, I think it is safe to say that you, and all with you have done honor to yourselves and the flag and service to the country. Most gratefully do I thank you and them. In my present position, I must care for the whole nation; but I hope it will be no injustice to any other state, for me to indulge a little home pride, that Illinois does not disappoint us.

I have just closed a long interview with Mr. Washburne in which he has detailed the many difficulties you, and those with you labor under. Be assured, we do not forget or neglect you. Much, very much, goes undone: but it is because we have not the power to do it faster than we do. Some of your forces are without arms, but the same is true here, and at every other place where we have considerable bodies of troops. The plain matter-of-fact is, our good people have rushed to the rescue of the Government, faster than the government can find arms to put into their hands.

It would be agreeable to each division of the army to know its own precise destination: but the Government cannot immediately, nor inflexibly at any time, determine as to all; nor if determined, can it tell its <u>friends</u> without at the same time telling its <u>enemies</u>.

We know you do all as wisely and well as you can; and you will not be deceived if you conclude the same is true of us. Please give my respects and thanks to all Yours very truly

A LINCOLN.

From *Collected Works*. Abraham Lincoln Association, Springfield, IL. Roy P. Basler, editor; Marion Dolores Pratt and Lloyd A. Dunlap, assistant editors. Lincoln, Abraham, 1809-1865. New Brunswick, N.J.: Rutgers University Press, 1953. Copyright © The Abraham Lincoln Association. Reprinted by permission.

To George B. McClellan, June 28, 1862

Washington City, D.C.
June 28--- 1862

Major Gen. McClellan

Save your Army at all events. Will send re-inforcements as fast as we can. Of course they can not reach you to-day, to-morrow, or next day. I have not said you were ungenerous for saying you needed re-inforcement. I thought you were ungenerous in assuming that I did not send them as fast as I could. I feel any misfortune to you and your Army quite as keenly as you feel it yourself. If you have had a drawn battle, or a repulse, it is the price we pay for the enemy not being in Washington. We protected Washington, and the enemy concentrated on you; had we stripped Washington, he would have been upon us before the troops sent could have got to you. Less than a week ago you notified us that re-inforcements were leaving Richmond to come in front of us. It is the nature of the case, and neither you or the government that is to blame. Please tell at once the present condition and aspect of things. A. LINCOLN

P.S. Gen. Pope thinks if you fall back, it would be much better towards York River, than towards the James. As Pope now has charge of the Capital, please confer with him through the telegraph. A. L.

To William H. Seward, June 28, 1862

Executive Mansion
June 28. 1862.

Hon. W. H. Seward

My dear Sir

My view of the present condition of the War is about as follows:

The evacuation of Corinth, and our delay by the flood in the Chicahominy, has enabled the enemy to concentrate too much force in Richmond for McClellan to successfully attack. In fact there soon will be no substantial rebel force any where else. But if we send all the force from here to McClellan, the enemy will, before we can know of it, send a force from Richmond and take Washington. Or, if a large part of the Western Army be brought here to McClellan, they will let us have Richmond, and retake Tennessee, Kentucky, Missouri &c. What should be done is to hold what we have in the West, open the Mississippi, and, take Chatanooga & East Tennessee, without more---a reasonable force should, in every event, be kept about Washington for it's protection. Then let the country give us a hundred thousand new troops in the shortest possible time, which added to McClellan, directly or indirectly, will take Richmond, without endangering any other place which we now hold---and will substantially end the war. I expect to maintain this contest until successful, or till I die, or am conquered, or my term expires, or Congress or the country forsakes me; and I would publicly appeal to the country for this new force, were it not that I fear a general panic and stampede would follow---so hard is it to have a thing understood as it really is. I think the new force should be all, or nearly all infantry, principally because such can be raised most cheaply and quickly. Yours very truly A. LINCOLN

To George B. McClellan, July 1, 1862

Executive Mansion,
Washington, July 1 1862.

Major Genl. McClellan---

It is impossible to re-inforce you for your present emergency. If we had a million of men we could not get them to you in time. We have not the men to send. If you are not strong enough to face the enemy you must find a place of security, and wait, rest, and repair. Maintain your ground if you can; but save the Army at all events, even if you fall back to Fortress-Monroe. We still have strength enough in the country, and will bring it out.

A. LINCOLN

To Joseph Hooker, January 26, 1863

Executive Mansion,
Washington, January 26, 1863.

Major General Hooker:

General.

I have placed you at the head of the Army of the Potomac. Of course I have done this upon what appear to me to be sufficient reasons. And yet I think it best for you to know that there are some things in regard to which, I am not quite satisfied with you. I believe you to be a brave and a skilful soldier, which, of course, I like. I also believe you do not mix politics with your profession, in which you are right. You have confidence in yourself, which is a valuable, if not an indispensable quality. You are ambitious, which, within reasonable bounds, does good rather than harm. But I think that during Gen. Burnside's command of the Army, you have taken counsel of your ambition, and thwarted him as much as you could, in which you did a great wrong to the country, and to a most meritorious and honorable brother officer. I have heard, in such way as to believe it, of your recently saying that both the Army and the Government needed a Dictator. Of course it was not for this, but in spite of it, that I have given you the command. Only those generals who gain successes, can set up dictators. What I now ask of you is military success, and I will risk the dictatorship. The government will support you to the utmost of it's ability, which is neither more nor less than it has done and will do for all commanders. I much fear that the spirit which you have aided to infuse into the Army, of criticising their Commander, and withholding confidence from him, will now turn upon you. I shall assist you as far as I can, to put it down. Neither you, nor Napoleon, if he were alive again, could get any good out of an army, while such a spirit prevails in it.

And now, beware of rashness. Beware of rashness, but with energy, and sleepless vigilance, go forward, and give us victories.

Yours very truly A. LINCOLN

To Joseph Hooker, June 10-14, 1863

[LTR To Joseph Hooker
United States Military Telegraph
"Cypher" War Department. Washington DC.

June 10. 1863. [6:40 P.M.]

Major General Hooker

Your long despatch of to-day is just received. If left to me, I would not go South of the Rappahannock, upon Lee's moving North of it. If you had Richmond invested to-day, you would not be able to take it in twenty days; meanwhile, your communications, and with them, your army would be ruined. I think Lee's Army, and not Richmond, is your true objective point. If he comes towards the Upper Potomac, follow on his flank, and on the inside track, shortening your lines, whilst he lengthens his. Fight him when oppertunity offers. If he stays where he is, fret him, and fret him. A LINCOLN

From *Collected Works*. Abraham Lincoln Association, Springfield, IL. Roy P. Basler, editor; Marion Dolores Pratt and Lloyd A. Dunlap, assistant editors. Lincoln, Abraham, 1809-1865. New Brunswick, N.J.: Rutgers University Press, 1953. Copyright © The Abraham Lincoln Association. Reprinted by permission.

To Joseph Hooker

Executive Mansion, Washington,
June 14. 11.55 P.M. 1863.

Major General Hooker.

Yours of 11.30 just received. You have nearly all the elements for forming an opinion whether Winchester is surrounded that I have. I really fear---almost believe, it is. No communication has been had with it during the day, either at Martinsburg, or Harper's Ferry. At 7 P.M., we also lost communication with Martinsburg.

The enemy had also appeared there some hours before. At 9. PM. Harper's Ferry said the enemy was reported at Berryville & Smithfield. If I could know that Longstreet and Ewell moved in that direction so long ago as you stated in your last, then I should feel sure that Winchester is strongly invested. It is quite certain that a considerable force of the enemy is thereabout; and I fear it is an overwhelming one, compared with Milroys. I am unable to give any more certain opinion. A. LINCOLN

From *Collected Works*. Abraham Lincoln Association, Springfield, IL. Roy P. Basler, editor; Marion Dolores Pratt and Lloyd A. Dunlap, assistant editors. Lincoln, Abraham, 1809-1865. New Brunswick, N.J.: Rutgers University Press, 1953. Copyright © The Abraham Lincoln Association. Reprinted by permission.

To Joseph Hooker

Washington City,
June 15. 8 1/2 P.M. 1863

Major General Hooker
Fairfax Station.

The facts are now known here that Winchester and Martinsburg were both besieged yesterday; the troops from Martinsburg have got into Harper's Ferry without loss; those from Winchester, are also in, having lost, in killed, wounded and missing, about one third of their number. Of course the enemy holds both places; and I think the report is authentic that he is crossing the Potomac at Williamsburg. We have not heard of his yet appearing at Harper's Ferry, or on the river anywhere below. I would like to hear from you. A. LINCOLN

From *Collected Works*. Abraham Lincoln Association, Springfield, IL. Roy P. Basler, editor; Marion Dolores Pratt and Lloyd A. Dunlap, assistant editors. Lincoln, Abraham, 1809-1865. New Brunswick, N.J.: Rutgers University Press, 1953. Copyright © The Abraham Lincoln Association. Reprinted by permission.

To Joseph Hooker

Washington, D.C.,
June 16, 1863.

Major General Hooker:
Your despatches of last night and this morning are just received. I shall have General Halleck to answer them carefully. Meanwhile, I can only say that, as I understand, Heintzelman commands here in this District; that what troops, or very nearly what number, are at Harper's Ferry I do not know, though I do know that Tyler is in command there. Your idea to send your cavalry to this side of the river may be right---probably is; still, it pains me a little that it looks like defensive merely, and seems to abandon the fair chance now presented of breaking the enemy's long and necessarily slim line, stretched now from the Rappahannock to Pennsylvania. A. LINCOLN.

From *Collected Works*. Abraham Lincoln Association, Springfield, IL. Roy P. Basler, editor; Marion Dolores Pratt and Lloyd A. Dunlap, assistant editors. Lincoln, Abraham, 1809-1865. New Brunswick, N.J.: Rutgers University Press, 1953. Copyright © The Abraham Lincoln Association. Reprinted by permission.

To Joseph Hooker

(Private.)

Executive Mansion, Washington, D.C.,
June 16, 1863.

My dear General: I send you this by the hand of Captain Dahlgren. Your despatch of 11:30 A.M. to-day is just received. When you say I have long been aware that you do not enjoy the confidence of the major-general commanding, you state the case much too strongly.

You do not lack his confidence in any degree to do you any harm. On seeing him, after telegraphing you this morning, I found him more nearly agreeing with you than I was myself. Surely you do not mean to understand that I am withholding my confidence from you when I happen to express an opinion (certainly never discourteously) differing from one of your own.

I believe Halleck is dissatisfied with you to this extent only, that he knows that you write and telegraph ("report," as he calls it) to me. I think he is wrong to find fault with this; but I do not think he withholds any support from you on account of it. If you and he would use the same frankness to one another, and to me, that I use to both of you, there would be no difficulty. I need and must have the professional skill of both, and yet these suspicions tend to deprive me of both.

I believe you are aware that since you took command of the army I have not believed you had any chance to effect anything till now. As it looks to me, Lee's now returning toward Harper's Ferry gives you back the chance that I thought McClellan lost last fall. Quite possibly I was wrong both then and now; but, in the great responsibility resting upon me, I cannot be entirely silent. Now, all I ask is that you will be in such mood that we can get into our action the best cordial judgment of yourself and General Halleck, with my poor mite added, if indeed he and you shall think it entitled to any consideration at all. Yours as ever,

A. LINCOLN.

From *Collected Works*. Abraham Lincoln Association, Springfield, IL. Roy P. Basler, editor; Marion Dolores Pratt and Lloyd A. Dunlap, assistant editors. Lincoln, Abraham, 1809-1865. New Brunswick, N.J.: Rutgers University Press, 1953. Copyright © The Abraham Lincoln Association. Reprinted by permission.

To Ulysses S. Grant, April 30, 1864

Executive Mansion Washington,
April 30, 1864

Lieutenant General Grant.

Not expecting to see you again before the Spring campaign opens, I wish to express, in this way, my entire satisfaction with what you have done up to this time, so far as I understand it. The particulars of your plans I neither know, or seek to know. You are vigilant and self-reliant; and, pleased with this, I wish not to obtrude any constraints or restraints upon you. While I am very anxious that any great disaster, or the capture of our men in great numbers, shall be avoided, I know these points are less likely to escape your attention than they would be mine. If there is anything wanting which is within my power to give, do not fail to let me know it.

And now with a brave Army, and a just cause, may God sustain you. Yours very truly A. LINCOLN

EXPLAINING THE COST

Resolving the constitutional issues surrounding secession and confronting generals who were at times overly-cautious and at other times overconfident, were not the only or even the most difficult challenges Lincoln faced as president. Equally tasking was the need to explain to those who had suffered great loss that their tremendous sacrifice was not without meaning. Even Lincoln himself was often hard-pressed to understand why the nation was being called upon to endure such a horrific toll as the war demanded. Lincoln apparently wrote the "Meditation on Divine Will" at a time when he was discouraged by the recent defeat of the Union army at Second Manassas, and struggling with the ramifications of a decision he had already made—the "weightiest question of his life" as he described it—to issue the Emancipation Proclamation. Two months later, Lincoln wrote a revealing letter to Fanny McCullough, a young girl whose father, Colonel William McCullough, had been killed at Coffeeville, Mississippi. Prior to the war, Colonel McCullough had served as the clerk of the McLean County Circuit Court in Illinois. Lincoln was well acquainted with him and, as he revealed in the letter to young Fanny, was also well acquainted with death. The death of his two sons, his sister, and his mother had allowed him a particular ability to empathize with those who were now called upon to endure a similar loss. Lincoln wrote several such letters of condolence, the best known of which was written to Mrs. Lydia Bixby near the end of the war. It has been speculated that Lincoln wrote only portions of the Bixby letter or perhaps outlined the letter for his secretary to complete. But the style and tone are both decidedly that of Lincoln and it is included here as an outstanding example of his empathy and compassion.

Lincoln was called upon to explain other aspects of the war as well, including his suspension of *Habeas corpus* and the nation's first conscription law, passed on March 3, 1863. The law established strict enlistment quotas, although volunteers counted toward the quota and reduced the number of men in each state who were subject to conscription. To assist with manpower requirements, Lincoln declared an amnesty for soldiers who were absent without leave and called upon all citizens to help enforce enlistments. The response to his call was lukewarm at best; in fact, there was much opposition to the conscription law. Erastus Corning, a prominent New York Democrat and the president of the New York Central Railroad, led a group that accused Lincoln of exercising powers usually reserved for monarchs and criticized him not only for conscription but also for the recent arrest of Clement Vallandingham, a prominent critic of Lincoln and the war. Lincoln responded on June 12, 1863, and made arrangements to have the letter published and available to the general public.

None of Lincoln's efforts to explain the war and its purpose is better known or more effective than the Gettysburg Address. He was invited to make "a few appropriate remarks" at the dedication of the new national cemetery on the Gettysburg Battlefield in November 1863. It was an opportunity to share with the country his belief that the struggles of the Civil War were not unrelated to the struggles that had first created the nation in 1776. Carefully worded and concise, his remarks were solemn enough to suit the occasion, yet sufficiently stirring to inspire confidence in the war and its objectives.

Meditation on the Divine Will, September 2, 1862 [?]

The will of God prevails. In great contests each party claims to act in accordance with the will of God. Both may be, and one must be wrong. God can not be for, and against the same thing at the same time. In the present civil war it is quite possible that God's purpose is something different from the purpose of either party---and yet the human instrumentalities, working just as they do, are of the best adaptation to effect His purpose. I am almost ready to say this is probably true---that God wills this contest, and wills that it shall not end yet. By his mere quiet power, on the minds of the now contestants, He could have either saved or destroyed the Union without a human contest. Yet the contest began. And having begun He could give the final victory to either side any day. Yet the contest proceeds.

From *Collected Works*. Abraham Lincoln Association, Springfield, IL. Roy P. Basler, editor; Marion Dolores Pratt and Lloyd A. Dunlap, assistant editors. Lincoln, Abraham, 1809-1865. New Brunswick, N.J.: Rutgers University Press, 1953. Copyright © The Abraham Lincoln Association. Reprinted by permission.

To Fanny McCullough, December 23, 1862

Executive Mansion,
Washington, December 23, 1862.

Dear Fanny
It is with deep grief that I learn of the death of your kind and brave Father; and, especially, that it is affecting your young heart beyond what is common in such cases. In this sad world of ours, sorrow comes to all; and, to the young, it comes with bitterest agony, because it takes them unawares. The older have learned to ever expect it. I am anxious to afford some alleviation of your present distress. Perfect relief is not possible, except with time. You can not now realize that you will ever feel better. Is not this so? And yet it is a mistake. You are sure to be happy again. To know this, which is certainly true, will make you some less miserable now. I have had experience enough to know what I say; and you need only to believe it, to feel better at once. The memory of your dear Father, instead of an agony, will yet be a sad sweet feeling in your heart, of a purer, and holier sort than you have known before.

Please present my kind regards to your afflicted mother.

Your sincere friend A. LINCOLN.

Miss. Fanny McCullough.

To Erastus Corning and Others, June 12, 1863

Executive Mansion
Washington [June 12] 1863.

Hon. Erastus Corning & others

Gentlemen Your letter of May 19th. inclosing the resolutions of a public meeting held at Albany, N.Y. on the 16th. of the same month, was received several days ago.

The resolutions, as I understand them, are resolvable into two propositions---first, the expression of a purpose to sustain the cause of the Union, to secure peace through victory, and to support the administration in every constitutional, and lawful measure to suppress the rebellion; and secondly, a declaration of censure upon the administration for supposed unconstitutional action such as the making of military arrests.

And, from the two propositions a third is deduced, which is, that the gentlemen composing the meeting are resolved on doing their part to maintain our common government and country, despite the folly or wickedness, as they may conceive, of any administration. This position is eminently patriotic, and as such, I thank the meeting, and congratulate the nation for it. My own purpose is the same; so that the meeting and myself have a common object, and can have no difference, except in the choice of means or measures, for effecting that object.

And here I ought to close this paper, and would close it, if there were no apprehension that more injurious consequences, than any merely personal to myself, might follow the censures systematically cast upon me for doing what, in my view of duty, I could not forbear. The resolutions promise to support me in every constitutional and lawful measure to suppress the rebellion; and I have not knowingly employed, nor shall knowingly employ, any other. But the meeting, by their resolutions, assert and argue, that certain military arrests and proceedings following them for which I am ultimately responsible, are unconstitutional. I think they are not. The resolutions quote from the constitution, the definition of treason; and also the limiting safe-guards and guarrantees therein provided for the citizen, on trials for treason, and on his being held to answer for capital or otherwise infamous crimes, and, in criminal prossecutions, his right to a speedy and public trial by an impartial jury. They proceed to resolve "That these safe-guards of the rights of the citizen against the pretentions of arbitrary power, were intended more <u>especially</u> for his protection in times of civil commotion." And, apparently, to demonstrate the proposition, the resolutions proceed "They were secured substantially to the English people, <u>after</u> years of protracted civil war, and were adopted into our constitution at the <u>close</u> of the revolution." Would not the demonstration have been better, if it could have been truly said that these safe-guards had been adopted, and applied <u>during</u> the civil wars and <u>during</u> our revolution, instead of <u>after</u> the one, and at the <u>close</u> of the other. I too am devotedly for them <u>after</u> civil war, and <u>before</u> civil war, and at all times "except when, in cases of Rebellion or Invasion, the public Safety may require" their suspension. The resolutions proceed to tell us that these safe-guards "have stood the test of seventysix years of trial, under our republican system, under circumstances which show that while they constitute the foundation of all free government, they are the elements of the enduring stability of the Republic." No one denies that they have so stood the test up to the beginning of the present rebellion if we except a certain matter [occurrence] at New-Orleans hereafter to be mentioned; nor does any one question that they will stand the same test much longer after the rebellion closes. But these provisions of the constitution have no application to the case we have in hand, because the arrests complained of were not made for treason---that is, not for <u>the</u> treason defined in the constitution, and upon the conviction of which, the punishment is death---- nor yet were they made to hold persons to answer for any capital, or otherwise infamous crimes; nor were the proceedings following, in any constitutional or legal sense, "criminal prossecutions." The arrests were made on totally different grounds, and the proceedings following, accorded with the grounds of the arrests. Let us consider the real case with which we are dealing, and apply to it the parts of the constitution plainly made for such cases.

Prior to my instalation here it had been inculcated that any State had a lawful right to secede from the national Union; and that it would be expedient to exercise the right, whenever the devotees of the doctrine should fail to elect a President to their own liking. I was elected contrary to their liking; and accordingly, so far as it was legally possible, they had taken seven states out of the Union, had seized many of the United States Forts, and had fired upon the United States' Flag, all before I was inaugerated; and, of course, before I had done any official act whatever. The rebellion, thus began soon ran into the present civil war; and, in certain respects, it began on very unequal terms between the parties. The insurgents had been preparing for it more than thirty years, while the government had taken no steps to resist them. The former had carefully considered all the means which could be turned to their account. It undoubtedly was a well pondered reliance with them that in their own unrestricted effort to destroy Union, constitution, and law, all together, the government would, in great degree, be restrained by the same constitution and law, from arresting their progress. Their sympathizers pervaded all departments of the government, and nearly all communities of the people. From this material, under cover of "Liberty of speech" "Liberty of the press" and "*Habeas corpus*" they hoped to keep on foot amongst us a most efficient corps of spies, informers, suppliers, and aiders and abettors of their cause in a thousand ways. They knew that in times such as they were inaugurating, by the constitution itself, the "*Habeas corpus*" might be suspended; but they also knew they had friends who would make a question as to <u>who</u> was to suspend it; meanwhile their spies and others might remain at large to help on their cause. Or if, as has happened, the executive should suspend the writ, without ruinous waste of time, instances of arresting innocent persons might occur, as are always likely to occur in such cases; and then a clamor could be raised in regard to this, which might be, at least, of some service to the insurgent cause. It needed no very keen perception to discover this part of the enemies' programme, so soon as by open hostilities their machinery was fairly put in motion. Yet, thoroughly imbued with a reverence for the guarranteed rights of individuals, I was slow to adopt the strong measures, which by degrees I have been forced to regard as being within the exceptions of the constitution, and as indispensable to the public Safety. Nothing is better known to history than that courts of justice are utterly incompetent to such cases. Civil courts are organized chiefly for trials of individuals, or, at most, a few individuals acting in concert; and this in quiet times, and on charges of crimes well defined in the law. Even in times of peace, bands of horse-thieves and robbers frequently grow too numerous and powerful for the ordinary courts of justice. But what comparison, in numbers, have such bands ever borne to the insurgent sympathizers even in many of the loyal states? Again, a jury too frequently have at least one member, more ready to hang the panel than to hang the traitor. And yet again, he who dissuades one man from volunteering, or induces one soldier to desert, weakens the Union cause as much as he who kills a union soldier in battle. Yet this dissuasion, or inducement, may be so conducted as to be no defined crime of which any civil court would take cognizance.

Ours is a case of Rebellion---so called by the resolutions before me---in fact, a clear, flagrant, and gigantic case of Rebellion; and the provision of the constitution that "The previlege of the writ of *Habeas Corpus* shall not be suspended, unless when in cases of Rebellion or Invasion, the public Safety may require it" is <u>the</u> provision which specially applies to our present case. This provision plainly attests the understanding of those who made the constitution that ordinary courts of justice are inadequate to "cases of Rebellion"---attests their purpose that in such cases, men may be held in custody whom the courts acting on ordinary rules, would discharge. *Habeas Corpus*, does not discharge men who are proved to be guilty of defined crime; and its suspension is allowed by the constitution on purpose that, men may be arrested and held, who can not be proved to be guilty of defined crime, "when, in cases of Rebellion or Invasion the public Safety may require it." This is precisely our present case---a case of Rebellion, wherein the public Safety does require the suspension. Indeed, arrests by process of courts, and arrests in cases of rebellion, do not proceed altogether upon the same basis. The former is directed at the small per centage of ordinary and continuous perpetration of crime; while the latter is directed at sudden and extensive uprisings against the government, which, at most, will succeed or fail, in no great length of time. In the latter case, arrests are made, not so much for what has been done, as for what probably would be done. The latter is more for the preventive, and less for the vindictive, than the former. In such cases the purposes of men are much more easily understood, than in cases of ordinary crime. The man who stands by and says nothing, when the peril of his government is discussed, can not be misunderstood. If not hindered, he is sure to help the enemy. Much more, if he talks ambiguously---talks for his country with "buts" and "ifs" and "ands." Of how little value the constitutional provision I have quoted will be rendered, if arrests shall never be made until defined crimes shall have been committed, may be illustrated by a few notable examples. Gen. John C. Breckienridge, Gen. Robert E. Lee, Gen. Joseph E. Johnston, Gen. John B. Magruder, Gen. William B. Preston, Gen. Simon B. Buckner, and Comodore [Franklin] Buchanan, now occupying the very highest places in the rebel war service, were all within the power of the government since the rebellion began, and were nearly as well known to be traitors then as now. Unquestionably if we had seized and held them, the insurgent cause would be much weaker. But no one of them had then committed any crime defined in the law. Every one of them if arrested would have been discharged on *Habeas Corpus*, were the writ allowed to operate. In view of these and similar cases, I think the time not unlikely to come when I shall be blamed for having made too few arrests rather than too many.

By the third resolution the meeting indicate their opinion that military arrests may be constitutional in localities where rebellion actually exists; but that such arrests are unconstitutional in localities where rebellion, or insurrection, does not actually exist. They insist that such arrests shall not be made "outside of the lines of necessary military occupation, and the scenes of insurrection" Inasmuch, however, as the constitution itself makes no such distinction, I am unable to believe that there is any such constitutional distinction. I concede that the class of arrests complained of, can be constitutional only when, in cases of Rebellion or Invasion, the public Safety may require them; and I insist that in such cases, they are constitutional <u>wherever</u> the public safety does require them---as well in places to which they may prevent the rebellion extending, as in those where it may be already prevailing---as well where they may restrain mischievous interference with the raising and supplying of armies, to suppress the rebellion, as where the rebellion may actually be---as well where they may restrain the enticing men out of the army, as where they would prevent mutiny in the army----equally constitutional at all places where they will conduce to the public Safety, as against the dangers of Rebellion or Invasion.

Take the particular case mentioned by the meeting. They assert [It is asserted] in substance that Mr. Vallandigham was by a military commander, seized and tried "for no other reason than words addressed to a public meeting, in criticism of the course of the administration, and in condemnation of the military orders of that general" Now, if there be no mistake about this---if this assertion is the truth and the whole truth---if there was no other reason for the arrest, then I concede that the arrest was wrong. But the arrest, as I understand, was made for a very different reason. Mr. Vallandigham avows his hostility to the war on the part of the Union; and his arrest was made because he was laboring, with some effect, to prevent the raising of troops, to encourage desertions from the army, and to leave the rebellion without an adequate military force to suppress it. He was not arrested because he was damaging the political prospects of the administration, or the personal interests of the commanding general; but because he was damaging the army, upon the existence, and vigor of which, the life of the nation depends. He was warring upon the military; and this gave the military constitutional jurisdiction to lay hands upon him. If Mr. Vallandigham was not damaging the military power of the country, then his arrest was made on mistake of fact, which I would be glad to correct, on reasonably satisfactory evidence.

I understand the meeting, whose resolutions I am considering, to be in favor of suppressing the rebellion by military force---by armies. Long experience has shown that armies can not be maintained unless desertion shall be punished by the severe penalty of death. The case requires, and the law and the constitution, sanction this punishment. Must I shoot a simple-minded soldier boy who deserts, while I must not touch a hair of a wiley agitator who induces him to desert? This is none the less injurious when effected by getting a father, or brother, or friend, into a public meeting, and there working upon his feeling, till he is persuaded to write the soldier boy, that he is fighting in a bad cause, for a wicked administration of a contemptable government, too weak to arrest and punish him if he shall desert. I think that in such a case, to silence the agitator, and save the boy, is not only constitutional, but, withal, a great mercy.

If I be wrong on this question of constitutional power, my error lies in believing that certain proceedings are constitutional when, in cases of rebellion or Invasion, the public Safety requires them, which would not be constitutional when, in absence of rebellion or invasion, the public Safety does not require them---in other words, that the constitution is not in it's application in all respects the same, in cases of Rebellion or invasion, involving the public Safety, as it is in times of profound peace and public security. The constitution itself makes the distinction; and I can no more be persuaded that the government can constitutionally take no strong measure in time of rebellion, because it can be shown that the same could not be lawfully taken in time of peace, than I can be persuaded that a particular drug is not good medicine for a sick man, because it can be shown to not be good food for a well one. Nor am I able to appreciate the danger, apprehended by the meeting, that the American people will, by means of military arrests during the rebellion, lose the right of public discussion, the liberty of speech and the press, the law of evidence, trial by jury, and *Habeas corpus*, throughout the indefinite peaceful future which I trust lies before them, any more than I am able to believe that a man could contract so strong an appetite for emetics during temporary illness, as to persist in feeding upon them through the remainder of his healthful life.

In giving the resolutions that earnest consideration which you request of me, I can not overlook the fact that the meeting speak as "Democrats." Nor can I, with full respect for their known intelligence, and the fairly presumed deliberation with which they prepared their resolutions, be permitted to suppose that this occurred by accident, or in any way other than that they preferred to designate themselves "democrats" rather than "American citizens." In this time of national peril I would have preferred to meet you upon a level one step higher than any party platform; because I am sure that from such more elevated position, we could do better battle for the country we all love, than we possibly can from those lower ones, where from the force of habit, the prejudices of the past, and selfish hopes of the future, we are sure to expend much of our ingenuity and strength, in finding fault with, and aiming blows at each other. But since you have denied me this, I will yet be thankful, for the country's sake, that not all democrats have done so. He on whose discretionary judgment Mr. Vallandigham was arrested and tried, is a democrat, having no old party affinity with me; and the judge who rejected the constitutional view expressed in these resolutions, by refusing to discharge Mr. V. on *Habeas Corpus*, is a democrat of better days than these, having received his judicial mantle at the hands of President Jackson. And still more, of all those democrats who are nobly exposing their lives and shedding their blood on the battle-field, I have learned that many approve the course taken with Mr. V. while I have not heard of a single one condemning it. I can not assert that there are none such.

And the name of President Jackson recalls a bit [an instance] of pertinent history. After the battle of New-Orleans, and while the fact that the treaty of peace had been concluded, was well known in the city, but before official knowledge of it had arrived, Gen. Jackson still maintained martial, or military law. Now, that it could be said the war was over, the clamor against martial law, which had existed from the first, grew more furious. Among other things a Mr. Louiallier published a denunciatory newspaper article. Gen. Jackson arrested him. A lawyer by the name of Morel procured the U.S. Judge Hall to order a writ of *Habeas Corpus* to release Mr. Louiallier. Gen. Jackson arrested both the lawyer and the judge. A Mr. Hollander ventured to say of some part of the matter that "it was a dirty trick." Gen. Jackson arrested him. When the officer undertook to serve the writ of *Habeas Corpus*, Gen. Jackson took it from him, and sent him away with a copy. Holding the judge in custody a few days, the general sent him beyond the limits of his encampment, and set him at liberty, with an order to remain till the ratification of peace should be regularly announced, or until the British should have left the Southern coast. A day or two more elapsed, the ratification of the treaty of peace was regularly announced, and the judge and others were fully liberated. A few days more, and the judge called Gen. Jackson into court and fined him a thousand dollars, for having arrested him and the others named. The general paid the fine, and there the matter rested for nearly thirty years, when congress refunded principal and interest. The late Senator Douglas, then in the House of Representatives, took a leading part in the debate, in which the constitutional question was much discussed. I am not prepared to say whom the Journals would show to have voted for the measure.

It may be remarked: First, that we had the same constitution then, as now. Secondly, that we then had a case of Invasion, and that now we have a case of Rebellion, and: Thirdly, that the permanent right of the people to public discussion, the liberty of speech and the press, the trial by jury, the law of evidence, and the *Habeas Corpus*, suffered no detriment whatever by that conduct of Gen. Jackson, or it's subsequent approval by the American congress.

And yet, let me say that in my own discretion, I do not know whether I would have ordered the arrest of Mr. V. While I can not shift the responsibility from myself, I hold that, as a general rule, the commander in the field is the better judge of the necessity in any particular case. Of course I must practice a general directory and revisory power in the matter.

One of the resolutions expresses the opinion of the meeting that arbitrary arrests will have the effect to divide and distract those who should be united in suppressing the rebellion; and I am specifically called on to discharge Mr. Vallandigham. I regard this as, at least, a fair appeal to me, on the expediency of exercising a constitutional power which I think exists. In response to such appeal I have to say it gave me pain when I learned that Mr. V. had been arrested,---that is, I was pained that there should have seemed to be a necessity for arresting him---and that it will afford me great pleasure to discharge him so soon as I can, by any means, believe the public safety will not suffer by it. I further say, that as the war progress, it appears to me, opinion, and action, which were in great confusion at first, take shape, and fall into more regular channels; so that the necessity for arbitrary [strong] dealing with them gradually decreases. I have every reason to desire that it would cease altogether; and far from the least is my regard for the opinions and wishes of those who, like the meeting at Albany, declare their purpose to sustain the government in every constitutional and lawful measure to suppress the rebellion. Still, I must continue to do so much as may seem to be required by the public safety. A. LINCOLN.

Address Delivered at the Dedication of the Cemetery at Gettysburg, November 19, 1863

Four score and seven years ago our fathers brought forth on this continent, a new nation, conceived in Liberty, and dedicated to the proposition that all men are created equal.

Now we are engaged in a great civil war, testing whether that nation, or any nation so conceived and so dedicated, can long endure. We are met on a great battle-field of that war. We have come to dedicate a portion of that field, as a final resting place for those who here gave their lives that that nation might live. It is altogether fitting and proper that we should do this.

But, in a larger sense, we can not dedicate---we can not consecrate---we can not hallow---this ground. The brave men, living and dead, who struggled here, have consecrated it, far above our poor power to add or detract. The world will little note, nor long remember what we say here, but it can never forget what they did here. It is for us the living, rather, to be dedicated here to the unfinished work which they who fought here have thus far so nobly advanced. It is rather for us to be here dedicated to the great task remaining before us---that from these honored dead we take increased devotion to that cause for which they gave the last full measure of devotion---that we here highly resolve that these dead shall not have died in vain---that this nation, under God, shall have a new birth of freedom---and that government of the people, by the people, for the people, shall not perish from the earth.

November 19. 1863. ABRAHAM LINCOLN.

To Mrs. Lydia Bixby, November 21, 1864.

Executive Mansion,
Washington, Nov. 21, 1864.

Dear Madam,---I have been shown in the files of the War Department a statement of the Adjutant General of Massachusetts, that you are the mother of five sons who have died gloriously on the field of battle.

I feel how weak and fruitless must be any words of mine which should attempt to beguile you from the grief of a loss so overwhelming. But I cannot refrain from tendering to you the consolation that may be found in the thanks of the Republic they died to save.

I pray that our Heavenly Father may assuage the anguish of your bereavement, and leave you only the cherished memory of the loved and lost, and the solemn pride that must be yours, to have laid so costly a sacrifice upon the altar of Freedom. Yours, very sincerely and respectfully, A. LINCOLN.

Mrs. Bixby.

LAST PHOTOGRAPH OF LINCOLN, MAY 1865

Library of Congress Prints and Photographs Division [LC-USZ62-12380].

REUNION AND RECONCILIATION

Lincoln steadfastly believed that if the people were willing to hold the course, Union victory was certain. As that victory approached, he also recognized that reconstructing the nation might prove to be more difficult than winning the war. The initial step in the process of reconstruction was to create loyal state governments as soon as possible, and the first chance to do so came in Tennessee. In a letter to newly appointed military governor Andrew Johnson, Lincoln reveals several concerns beyond the need for haste and loyalty. By December of that year, Lincoln was prepared to announce a policy for the treatment of those who had taken part in the rebellion and released the "Proclamation of Amnesty and Reconstruction." While the proclamation outlined clear provisions, particularly relating to slave property, Lincoln was prepared to pardon and grant amnesty to those men who signed an oath of allegiance to the United States. Lincoln approached reconstruction with conciliation and some measure of forgiveness for those who had participated in the rebellion. In fact, he soon came to believe that such an approach offered the best hope of restoring the Union with a minimum amount of bitterness and resentment. Two months later, the document provided the authority for a gubernatorial election in Louisiana in which Michael Hahn, a New Orleans Unionist, was elected governor. Lincoln congratulated Hahn for winning the election, in which only 11,000 votes had been cast, and then suggested to the new governor that future elections ought to extend the suffrage to qualified Black voters, particularly those who had served in the Union army. By the time Lincoln wrote this letter, however, he knew that Black suffrage was not popular, nor for that matter was the war. There was a growing national perception that the war had devolved into an unwinnable stalemate, and Lincoln genuinely feared that he could not win re-election, as indicated in his "Memorandum Concerning the Probable Failure of Re-election." Those fears proved unfounded, and with Lincoln's re-election in 1864, he was free to pursue some of his controversial measures more aggressively. At the heart of his vision for the future was the belief that the bitterness of the war must be forgotten for the reunited nation to function effectively. His Second Inaugural Address states this belief eloquently and simply. Far less eloquent was Lincoln's final public address on April 11, 1865. It was delivered from a balcony of the White House in response to a serenading crowd still celebrating the capture of Richmond and the surrender of Confederate General Robert E. Lee. The crowd certainly expected Lincoln to join in the celebration, but he chose instead to discuss what was most important to him: the character and qualities that he envisioned for the reconstructed nation, among which was some form of Black suffrage. His speech that night was apparently not well received—many of his listeners wandered off long before the speech was over. But one person who was in the crowd that night understood exactly what Lincoln envisioned for the reunited nation, and the prospect so enraged him that he remarked to a friend, "that is the last speech he will ever make." Three days later, John Wilkes Booth made good on his promise.

To Andrew Johnson, September 11, 1863

Executive Mansion, Washington,
September 11, 1863.

Private
Hon. Andrew Johnson:

My dear Sir:

All Tennessee is now clear of armed insurrectionists. You need not to be reminded that it is the nick of time for re-inaugerating a loyal State government. Not a moment should be lost. You, and the co-operating friends there, can better judge of the ways and means, than can be judged by any here. I only offer a few suggestions. The re-inaugeration must not be such as to give control of the State, and it's representation in Congress, to the enemies of the Union, driving it's friends there into political exile. The whole struggle for Tennessee will have been profitless to both State and Nation, if it so ends that Gov. Johnson is put down, and Gov. Harris is put up. It must not be so. You must have it otherwise. Let the reconstruction be the work of such men only as can be trusted for the Union. Exclude all others, and trust that your government, so organized, will be recognized here, as being the one of republican form, to be guarranteed to the state, and to be protected against invasion and domestic violence.

It is something on the question of <u>time</u>, to remember that it can not be known who is next to occupy the position I now hold, nor what he will do.

I see that you have declared in favor of emancipation in Tennessee, for which, may God bless you. Get emancipation into your new State government---Constitution---and there will be no such word as fail for your case.

The raising of colored troops I think will greatly help every way. Yours very truly
A. LINCOLN

Proclamation of Amnesty and Reconstruction, December 8, 1863

By the President of the United States of America:

A Proclamation.

Whereas, in and by the Constitution of the United States, it is provided that the President "shall have power to grant reprieves and pardons for offences against the United States, except in cases of impeachment;" and

Whereas a rebellion now exists whereby the loyal State governments of several States have for a long time been subverted, and many persons have committed and are now guilty of treason against the United States; and

Whereas, with reference to said rebellion and treason, laws have been enacted by Congress declaring forfeitures and confiscation of property and liberation of slaves, all upon terms and conditions therein stated, and also declaring that the President was thereby authorized at any time thereafter, by proclamation, to extend to persons who may have participated in the existing rebellion, in any State or part thereof, pardon and amnesty, with such exceptions and at such times and on such conditions as he may deem expedient for the public welfare; and

Whereas the congressional declaration for limited and conditional pardon accords with well-established

Whereas, with reference to said rebellion, the President of the United States has issued several proclamations, with provisions in regard to the liberation of slaves; and

Whereas it is now desired by some persons heretofore engaged in said rebellion to resume their allegiance to the United States, and to reinaugurate loyal State governments within and for their respective States; therefore,

I, Abraham Lincoln, President of the United States, do proclaim, declare, and make known to all persons who have, directly or by implication, participated in the existing rebellion, except as hereinafter excepted, that a full pardon is hereby granted to them and each of them, with restoration of all rights of property, except as to slaves, and in property cases where rights of third parties shall have intervened, and upon the condition that every such person shall take and subscribe an oath, and thenceforward keep and maintain said oath inviolate; and which oath shall be registered for permanent preservation, and shall be of the tenor and effect following, to wit:

"I, ---, do solemnly swear, in presence of Almighty God, that I will henceforth faithfully support, protect and defend the Constitution of the United States, and the union of the States thereunder; and that I will, in like manner, abide by and faithfully support all acts of Congress passed during the existing rebellion with reference to slaves, so long and so far as not repealed, modified or held void by Congress, or by decision of the Supreme Court; and that I will, in like manner, abide by and faithfully support all proclamations of the President made during the existing rebellion having reference to slaves, so long and so far as not modified or declared void by decision of the Supreme Court. So help me God."

The persons excepted from the benefits of the foregoing provisions are all who are, or shall have been, civil or diplomatic officers or agents of the so-called confederate government; all who have left judicial stations under the United States to aid the rebellion; all who are, or shall have been, military or naval officers of said so-called confederate government above the rank of colonel in the army, or of lieutenant in the navy; all who left seats in the United States Congress to aid the rebellion; all who resigned commissions in the army or navy of the United States, and afterwards aided the rebellion; and all who have engaged in any way in treating colored persons or white persons, in charge of such, otherwise than lawfully as prisoners of war, and which persons may have been found in the United States service, as soldiers, seamen, or in any other capacity.

And I do further proclaim, declare, and make known, that whenever, in any of the States of Arkansas, Texas, Louisiana, Mississippi, Tennessee, Alabama, Georgia, Florida, South Carolina, and North Carolina, a number of persons, not less than one-tenth in number of the votes cast in such State at the Presidential election of the year of our Lord one thousand eight hundred and sixty, each having taken the oath aforesaid and not having since violated it, and being a qualified voter by the election law of the State existing immediately before the so-called act of secession, and excluding all others, shall re-establish a State government which shall be republican, and in no wise contravening said oath, such shall be recognized as the true government of the State, and the State shall receive thereunder the benefits of the constitutional provision which declares that "The United States shall guaranty to every State in this union a republican form of government, and shall protect each of them against invasion; and, on application of the legislature, or the executive, (when the legislature cannot be convened,) against domestic violence."

And I do further proclaim, declare, and make known that any provision which may be adopted by such State government in relation to the freed people of such State, which shall recognize and declare their permanent freedom, provide for their education, and which may yet be consistent, as a temporary arrangement, with their present condition as a laboring, landless, and homeless class, will not be objected to by the national Executive. And it is suggested as not improper, that, in constructing a loyal State government in any State, the name of the State, the boundary, the subdivisions, the constitution, and the general code of laws, as before the rebellion, be maintained, subject only to the modifications made necessary by the conditions hereinbefore stated, and such others, if any, not contravening said conditions, and which may be deemed expedient by those framing the new State government.

To avoid misunderstanding, it may be proper to say that this proclamation, so far as it relates to State governments, has no reference to States wherein loyal State governments have all the while been maintained. And for the same reason, it may be proper to further say that whether members sent to Congress from any State shall be admitted to seats, constitutionally rests exclusively with the respective Houses, and not to any extent with the Executive. And still further, that this proclamation is intended to present the people of the States wherein the national authority has been suspended, and loyal State governments have been subverted, a mode in and by which the national authority and loyal State governments may be re-established within said States, or in any of them; and, while the mode presented is the best the Executive can suggest, with his present impressions, it must not be understood that no other possible mode would be acceptable.

[L.S.]
Given under my hand at the city, of Washington, the 8th. day of December, A.D. one thousand eight hundred and sixty-three, and of the independence of the United States of America the eighty-eighth. ABRAHAM LINCOLN
By the President:
WILLIAM H. SEWARD, Secretary of State.

To Michael Hahn, March 13. 1864

Washington, Executive Mansion,
March 13. 1864.
Private

Hon. Michael Hahn

My dear Sir:

I congratulate you on having fixed your name in history as the first-free-state Governor of Louisiana. Now you are about to have a Convention which, among other things, will probably define the elective franchise. I barely suggest for your private consideration, whether some of the colored people may not be let in---as, for instance, the very intelligent, and especially those who have fought gallantly in our ranks. They would probably help, in some trying time to come, to keep the jewel of liberty within the family of freedom. But this is only a suggestion, not to the public, but to you alone. Yours truly A. LINCOLN

Memorandum Concerning His Probable Failure of Re-election,
August 23, 1864

Executive Mansion
Washington, Aug. 23, 1864.

This morning, as for some days past, it seems exceedingly probable that this Administration will not be re-elected. Then it will be my duty to so co-operate with the President elect, as to save the Union between the election and the inauguration; as he will have secured his election on such ground that he can not possibly save it afterwards. A. LINCOLN

Second Inaugural Address, March 4, 1865

Fellow Countrymen:

At this second appearing to take the oath of the presidential office, there is less occasion for an extended address than there was at the first. Then a statement, somewhat in detail, of a course to be pursued, seemed fitting and proper. Now, at the expiration of four years, during which public declarations have been constantly called forth on every point and phase of the great contest which still absorbs the attention, and engrosses the enerergies [sic] of the nation, little that is new could be presented. The progress of our arms, upon which all else chiefly depends, is as well known to the public as to myself; and it is, I trust, reasonably satisfactory and encouraging to all. With high hope for the future, no prediction in regard to it is ventured.

On the occasion corresponding to this four years ago, all thoughts were anxiously directed to an impending civil-war. All dreaded it---all sought to avert it. While the inaugeral address was being delivered from this place, devoted altogether to saving the Union without war, insurgent agents were in the city seeking to destroy it without war---seeking to dissol[v]e the Union, and divide effects, by negotiation. Both parties deprecated war; but one of them would make war rather than let the nation survive; and the other would accept war rather than let it perish. And the war came.

One eighth of the whole population were colored slaves, not distributed generally over the Union, but localized in the Southern part of it. These slaves constituted a peculiar and powerful interest. All knew that this interest was, somehow, the cause of the war. To strengthen, perpetuate, and extend this interest was the object for which the insurgents would rend the Union, even by war; while the government claimed no right to do more than to restrict the territorial enlargement of it. Neither party expected for the war, the magnitude, or the duration, which it has already attained. Neither anticipated that the cause of the conflict might cease with, or even before, the conflict itself should cease. Each looked for an easier triumph, and a result less fundamental and astounding. Both read the same Bible, and pray to the same God; and each invokes His aid against the other. It may seem strange that any men should dare to ask a just God's assistance in wringing their bread from the sweat of other men's faces; but let us judge not that we be not judged. The prayers of both could not be answered; that of neither has been answered fully. The Almighty has His own purposes. "Woe unto the world because of offences! for it must needs be that offences come; but woe to that man by whom the offence cometh!" If we shall suppose that American Slavery is one of those offences which, in the providence of God, must needs come, but which, having continued through His appointed time, He now wills to remove, and that He gives to both North and South, this terrible war, as the woe due to those by whom the offence came, shall we discern therein any departure from those divine attributes which the believers in a Living God always ascribe to Him? Fondly do we hope---fervently do we pray---that this mighty scourge of war may speedily pass away. Yet, if God wills that it continue, until all the wealth piled by the bond-man's two hundred and fifty years of unrequited toil shall be sunk, and until every drop of blood drawn with the lash, shall be paid by another drawn with the sword, as was said three thousand years ago, so still it must be said "the judgments of the Lord, are true and righteous altogether."

With malice toward none; with charity for all; with firmness in the right, as God gives us to see the right, let us strive on to finish the work we are in; to bind up the nation's wounds; to care for him who shall have borne the battle, and for his widow, and his orphan---to do all which may achieve and cherish a just, and a lasting peace, among ourselves, and with all nations.

[Endorsement]

Original manuscript of second Inaugeral presented to Major John Hay. A. LINCOLN

April 10. 1865

Last Public Address, April 11, 1865

We meet this evening, not in sorrow, but in gladness of heart. The evacuation of Petersburg and Richmond, and the surrender of the principal insurgent army, give hope of a righteous and speedy peace whose joyous expression can not be restrained. In the midst of this, however, He, from Whom all blessings flow, must not be forgotten. A call for a national thanksgiving is being prepared, and will be duly promulgated. Nor must those whose harder part gives us the cause of rejoicing, be overlooked. Their honors must not be parcelled out with others. I myself, was near the front, and had the high pleasure of transmitting much of the good news to you; but no part of the honor, for plan or execution, is mine. To Gen. Grant, his skilful officers, and brave men, all belongs. The gallant Navy stood ready, but was not in reach to take active part.

By these recent successes the re-inauguration of the national authority---reconstruction---which has had a large share of thought from the first, is pressed much more closely upon our attention. It is fraught with great difficulty. Unlike the case of a war between independent nations, there is no authorized organ for us to treat with. No one man has authority to give up the rebellion for any other man. We simply must begin with, and mould from, disorganized and discordant elements. Nor is it a small additional embarrassment that we, the loyal people, differ among ourselves as to the mode, manner, and means of reconstruction.

As a general rule, I abstain from reading the reports of attacks upon myself, wishing not to be provoked by that to which I can not properly offer an answer. In spite of this precaution, however, it comes to my knowledge that I am much censured for some supposed agency in setting up, and seeking to sustain, the new State Government of Louisiana. In this I have done just so much as, and no more than, the public knows. In the Annual Message of Dec. 1863 and accompanying Proclamation, I presented a plan of re-construction (as the phrase goes) which, I promised, if adopted by any State, should be acceptable to, and sustained by, the Executive government of the nation. I distinctly stated that this was not the only plan which might possibly be acceptable; and I also distinctly protested that the Executive claimed no right to say when, or whether members should be admitted to seats in Congress from such States. This plan was, in advance, submitted to the then Cabinet, and distinctly approved by every member of it. One of them suggested that I should then, and in that connection, apply the Emancipation Proclamation to the theretofore excepted parts of

Virginia and Louisiana; that I should drop the suggestion about apprenticeship for freed-people, and that I should omit the protest against my own power, in regard to the admission of members to Congress; but even he approved every part and parcel of the plan which has since been employed or touched by the action of Louisiana. The new constitution of Louisiana, declaring emancipation for the whole State, practically applies the Proclamation to the part previously excepted. It does not adopt apprenticeship for freed-people; and it is silent, as it could not well be otherwise, about the admission of members to Congress. So that, as it applies to Louisiana, every member of the Cabinet fully approved the plan. The Message went to Congress, and I received many commendations of the plan, written and verbal; and not a single objection to it, from any professed emancipationist, came to my knowledge, until after the news reached Washington that the people of Louisiana had begun to move in accordance with it. From about July 1862, I had corresponded with different persons, supposed to be interested, seeking a reconstruction of a State government for Louisiana. When the Message of 1863, with the plan before mentioned, reached New-Orleans, Gen. Banks wrote me that he was confident the people, with his military co-operation, would reconstruct, substantially on that plan. I wrote him, and some of them to try it; they tried it, and the result is known. Such only has been my agency in getting up the Louisiana government. As to sustaining it, my promise is out, as before stated. But, as bad promises are better broken than kept, I shall treat this as a bad promise, and break it, whenever I shall be convinced that keeping it is adverse to the public interest. But I have not yet been so convinced.

I have been shown a letter on this subject, supposed to be an able one, in which the writer expresses regret that my mind has not seemed to be definitely fixed on the question whether the seceded States, so called, are in the Union or out of it. It would perhaps, add astonishment to his regret, were he to learn that since I have found professed Union men endeavoring to make that question, I have purposely forborne any public expression upon it. As appears to me that question has not been, nor yet is, a practically material one, and that any discussion of it, while it thus remains practically immaterial, could have no effect other than the mischievous one of dividing our friends. As yet, whatever it may hereafter become, that question is bad, as the basis of a controversy, and good for nothing at all---a merely pernicious abstraction.

We all agree that the seceded States, so called, are out of their proper practical relation with the Union; and that the sole object of the government, civil and military, in regard to those States is to again get them into that proper practical relation. I believe it is not only possible, but in fact, easier, to do this, without deciding, or even considering, whether these states have even been out of the Union, than with it. Finding themselves safely at home, it would be utterly immaterial whether they had ever been abroad. Let us all join in doing the acts necessary to restoring the proper practical relations between these states and the Union; and each forever after, innocently indulge his own opinion whether, in doing the acts, he brought the States from without, into the Union, or only gave them proper assistance, they never having been out of it.

The amount of constituency, so to [sic] speak, on which the new Louisiana government rests, would be more satisfactory to all, if it contained fifty, thirty, or even twenty thousand, instead of only about twelve thousand, as it does. It is also unsatisfactory to some that the elective franchise is not given to the colored man. I would myself prefer that it were now conferred on the very intelligent, and on those who serve our cause as soldiers. Still the question is not whether the Louisiana government, as it stands, is quite all that is desirable. The question is "Will it be wiser to take it as it is, and help to improve it; or to reject, and disperse it?" "Can Louisiana be brought into proper practical relation with the Union sooner by sustaining, or by discarding her new State Government?"

Some twelve thousand voters in the heretofore slave-state of Louisiana have sworn allegiance to the Union, assumed to be the rightful political power of the State, held elections, organized a State government, adopted a free-state constitution, giving the benefit of public schools equally to black and white, and empowering the Legislature to confer the elective franchise upon the colored man. Their Legislature has already voted to ratify the constitutional amendment recently passed by Congress, abolishing slavery throughout the nation. These twelve thousand persons are thus fully committed to the Union, and to perpetual freedom in the state---committed to the very things, and nearly all the things the nation wants---and they ask the nations recognition, and it's assistance to make good their committal. Now, if we reject, and spurn them, we do our utmost to disorganize and disperse them. We in effect say to the white men "You are worthless, or worse---we will neither help you, nor be helped by you." To the blacks we say "This cup of liberty which these, your old masters, hold to your lips, we will dash from you, and leave you to the chances of gathering the spilled and scattered contents in some vague and undefined when, where, and how." If this course, discouraging and paralyzing both white and black, has any tendency to bring Louisiana into proper practical relations with the Union, I have, so far, been unable to perceive it. If, on the contrary, we recognize, and sustain the new government of Louisiana the converse of all this is made true. We encourage the hearts, and nerve the arms of the twelve thousand to adhere to their work, and argue for it, and proselyte for it, and fight for it, and feed it, and grow it, and ripen it to a complete success. The colored man too, in seeing all united for him, is inspired with vigilance, and energy, and daring, to the same end. Grant that he desires the elective franchise, will he not attain it sooner by saving the already advanced steps toward it, than by running backward over them? Concede that the new government of Louisiana is only to what it should be as the egg is to the fowl, we shall sooner have the fowl by hatching the egg than by smashing it? Again, if we reject Louisiana, we also reject one vote in favor of the proposed amendment to the national constitution. To meet this proposition, it has been argued that no more than three fourths of those States which have not attempted secession are necessary to validly ratify the amendment. I do not commit myself against this, further than to say that such a ratification would be questionable, and sure to be persistently questioned; while a ratification by three fourths of all the States would be unquestioned and unquestionable.

I repeat the question. "Can Louisiana be brought into proper practical relation with the Union sooner by sustaining or by discarding her new State Government?

What has been said of Louisiana will apply generally to other States. And yet so great peculiarities pertain to each state; and such important and sudden changes occur in the same state; and, withal, so new and unprecedented is the whole case, that no exclusive, and inflexible plan can safely be prescribed as to details and colatterals. Such exclusive, and inflexible plan, would surely become a new entanglement. Important principles may, and must, be inflexible.

In the present "situation" as the phrase goes, it may be my duty to make some new announcement to the people of the South. I am considering, and shall not fail to act, when satisfied that action will be proper.

CPSIA information can be obtained
at www.ICGtesting.com
Printed in the USA
LVOW02s1155170716
496095LV00006B/22/P